ABSURDLY STRANGE
BUT TRUE

WEIRD, CRAZY AND STRAIGHT OUT
OUTRAGEOUS FACTS AND STORIES THAT
YOU WON'T BELIEVE ARE TRUE!

BILL O'NEILL

ISBN-13: 978-1-64845-085-3

Copyright © 2022 by LAK Publishing

DON'T FORGET YOUR FREE BOOKS

CONTENTS

INTRODUCTION

Did you know that the concept of 'animal magnetism' is based on a real scientific theory? Have you ever wondered why cats always seem to find their way home? Do you think that some things in the world are truly amazing but also absurd?

If you've answered yes to any of these questions, then *Absurdly Strange But True* is the book for you!

In this book, you'll read about some of the craziest, zaniest, and most unbelievable stories known to humans, but as unbelievable as many of them may seem, I guarantee you that each story is 100% factual!

This book is organized into six chapters by subject - history, pop culture and sports, science, literature and art, geography, and the unexplained - with eight stories in each chapter, so there's sure to be something here for everyone.

At the end of each chapter are a series of ten "Strange but True" facts that concern that chapter's topic.

The arrangement of this book is a big part of what makes it so fun. You can pick and choose a chapter, or story, and move around the book, back and forth. This book is also a great ice breaker and conversation piece. Break it out the next time friends come by your house or take it with you when you visit family during the holidays.

I guarantee that everyone there will have a great time reading it.

I can also guarantee that you'll likely find yourself reading all of this book, even the chapters of subjects that may not normally interest you. This isn't your average history, science, or art book, full of boring facts, dry language, and a lot of jargon that's hard to follow. No, this is a book written with everyone in mind in a way that will keep you interested and wanting to read more.

Some of these stories will make you scratch your head, while others will make you say "WFT" or "Lol," but they're all sure to entertain you. So, sit back and enjoy, relax, and open your mind to the world as you've never before seen it.

CHAPTER 1:

ABSURD HISTORY

History is usually taught from the perspective of great men and women who led armies, nations, and political movements to effect great change throughout the world. After all, there's some truth to the adage that "history is written by the winners," and the winners are usually those who gloriously (at least in their minds) won battles, elections, invented things, etc.

But there have also been several absurd, weird, and bizarre events that have played major roles in history. Some of these people and events were part of bigger, better-known events, and their more absurd details have been relegated to footnotes of history books if even that. Because a couple of these were obscure events, to begin with, they've been the subject of very few discussions, but they later gained more interest and found themselves in journals, magazines, and books, such as this one.

Whatever the case, all of these eight stories, taken from some very different points in history from around the world, show that history may be written by the victors, but it's often made by the absurd.

Hooking for the Gods

You've probably heard the expression, "history's oldest profession" with reference to prostitution or sex work, as it is now more commonly known. And although there's no evidence the Neanderthals or Cro-Magnons had the practice of sex work, the earliest documented evidence of it dates to around 5,000 years ago with the dawn of civilization.

Yes, that's right, when humans started living in cities, developing writing, and creating sophisticated religions and governments, sex work was not far behind. The weird and absurd thing about it is that the earliest documented sex work was directly connected to religion.

You read the correctly - ancient hookers turned tricks for their gods!

This very unique form of sex work can be traced back to ancient Mesopotamia, which is where the modern country of Iraq is located. The ancient Sumerians worshipped plenty of gods and goddesses, but at the head of their pantheon was a female deity named Inanna, who was the goddess of love and war.

After the Sumerians lost power in Mesopotamia in the late 3rd millennium BCE, other groups in the region - such as the Akkadians, Kassites, and Assyrians - worshipped Inanna by her Akkadian name, Ishtar.

But whether she was known as Inanna or Ishtar, she was a goddess who was a bit on the freaky side!

Modern archaeologists believe that the sex work took place right in the Ishtar/Inanna temples and that the temple sex workers were respected members of the priestess class.

So, how were these women paid for their services?

The 5th-century BCE Greek historian, Herodotus, offers an interesting anecdote of the process:

> *"Once a woman has taken her seat she is not allowed to go home until a man has thrown a silver coin into her lap and taken her outside to lie with her. . . The value of the coin is of no consequence; once thrown it becomes sacred, and the law forbids that it should ever be refused."*

It's important to point out that when temple sex work began in Mesopotamia sometime after 3000 BCE, there were no coins. So, before the 6th century BCE, when coinage began to become prevalent in the Near East, the sex workers' clients would've probably paid with a variety of items.

Chickens, wheat, linen, and even blocks of silver all would've been brought to the temple for the customer to have his fun.

It's important to point out that Ishtar was usually among the two or three most important deities of the various people who ruled ancient Mesopotamia. No doubt part of that was because of her warlike nature, and how she was depicted in myths and religious texts as a protector of her people.

But I think it'd also be safe to say that Ishtar's popularity was due in large part to her association with love, fertility, and sex.

At first, it may seem strange to our modern sentiments to think of a goddess who was the patron of love *and* war, and even stranger that ritualized sex work was done to appease this goddess. But maybe it isn't so absurd when you really think about it.

Since the dawn of humanity, people have been killing each other, but they've also been making love, so in some ways, the people of ancient Mesopotamia were probably on to something!

335 Years Is an Absurdly Long Time for a War

Some pretty serious wars in world history had some pretty long spans. World War II was six years, but closer to 15 years if you count the Japanese invasion of Manchuria. More than a decade is a long time for a war, especially when millions were killed.

But World War II doesn't have anything on the Thirty Years' War.

The Thirty Years' War was a religious war fought between Protestant and Catholic kingdoms in what is today Germany from 1618 to 1648. Up to eight million people died in that war and untold fields and cities were destroyed in a conflict that really didn't settle much of anything.

But as absurd as that is, the Hundred Years' War was even crazier.

From 1337 to 1453, so actually a little more than 100 Years, France and England fought for control of the French throne and lands in France. Since the war lasted so long, no one who fought in its later stages was even born yet when it began! For that matter, when you consider the fact that average life expectancy was quite a bit lower back then, it's doubtful anyone man who fought until the end of the war had an ancestor still living from when the war started.

That's pretty amazing when you really sit and think about it, and even more so when you consider that, with limited technology and literacy in the 15th century, most of the men fighting didn't even know *why* they were fighting, other than their king ordered them to do so.

The term "Hundred Years' War" was a later term invented by historians to describe the series of events which included 3 phrases of war and peace – The Edwardian War (1337-1360), The Caroline War (1369-1389) and the Lancastrian War (1415-145j8). So yes, 100 years is an absurdly long time for a war, but 335 years of warfare definitely wins the prize.

The Three Hundred- and Thirty-Five-Years' War is one of those quirks of history that are easily forgotten, but since it was so strange, it's more than worthy of mention in this book.

The war began on March 1651, when Oliver Cromwell and his Parliamentarian army were wrapping up their victory against the Royalists in the English Civil War (1642-1651). When it became clear that the Parliamentarians were going to win and heads would roll, literally, a group of Royalists led by John Grenville fled to the Isles of Scilly.

That's Scilly, not Sicily.

"What and where's Scilly?" you're probably thinking? The Isles of Scilly are a small archipelago located about 28 miles off the tip of Cornwall, which is the far southeastern tip of England. Today the combined population of the isles is just over 2,000, and it was considerably less in the 1600s.

In other words, it's about as isolated a location in the British Isles as can be. It was so isolated that it wasn't until the end of the war that the Parliamentarians and their Dutch allies, who had declared war on Scilly, took the archipelago by force. Dutch Admiral Maarten Tromp demanded payment for having to come to the isolated islands and fired a few shots, and when he didn't receive said payment, he promptly declared war on Scilly but left, never to return.

So, the Isles of Scilly and the Netherlands were in a bizarre, quasi-state of war from 1651 onward. But it was a state of war that few people took seriously.

7

Grenville was imprisoned at the end of the war by the Parliamentarian forces but was later released. Although he continued to support the Royalist cause, he forgot about the Isles of Scilly.

The Dutch also forgot about the Isles of Scilly, and so did everyone else for the most part -except for the few people and plenty of sheep living on the archipelago!

It wasn't until 1986 that historians and political leaders rediscovered Scilly and the Netherlands were technically at war. An official peace treaty was signed that year, but some historians and political scientists don't even think it was necessary. They argue that a peace treaty technically couldn't be signed since the Isles of Scilly were never a sovereign nation and Tromp was acting on his own, apart from the Dutch government.

Perhaps that just shows how bizarre the whole thing was and that as awful and destructive as wars can be, they can also be quite absurd.

One of Britain's Greatest Explorers Was Also a Pirate

One of the features of modern society/civilization is how rules are applied to almost everything. This includes taxes, local, state, and federal laws - which sometimes are seemingly contradictory - and a host of regulations aimed at businesses. The regulation trend has also been applied to war.

There have been a series of international agreements relating to war, most notably the Geneva Convention of 1949. These modern "rules of war" generally outlaw the targeting of civilian populations by any military power to prevent things like robbery, rape, and genocide. Many people believe they are a good thing and a reflection of enlightened, modern society, while others believe it's simply absurd to have "rules of war."

The truth is, though, that these modern rules of war weren't invented suddenly in the 20th century but came about hundreds of years earlier in somewhat absurd circumstances.

The 1500s was a time of transition in Europe. The Reformation was changing the social fabric and the discovery of the "New World" was bringing immense wealth back to the continent. And, of course, whenever there's a lot of money involved, there's also sure to be some conflict.

As more lands and wealth were discovered in the Americas, pirates started to get in on the action, which is where we start to get into the absurd and the wild background of our next subject.

All of the major European powers at the time frowned on piracy, *officially*. It was, however, a very lucrative endeavor for those involved, so by the mid-1500s, the rulers of Europe developed a clever - and arguably absurd - workaround known as "privateers."

Privateers were simply pirates who did their theft under a nation's flag. In theory, the flag protected them from summary execution if captured, but that wasn't always the case, which brings us to Francis Drake.

Today, Francis Drake, often referred to by his knighted title, "Sir Francis Drake," is seen as a hero of British history - an intrepid, heroic explorer who was the first person to lead a circumnavigation of the globe the entire way.

But as great as Drake's accomplishments may have been, his explorations were little more than glorified pirate raids.

Drake's life began in 1540 to a common English family, but by the time he was 20, he had distinguished himself as a skilled sailor.

Once Drake became captain of his own ship at the age of 22 and began his career as a merchant, it didn't take the young man long to learn where the real money was.

Drake became involved in the slave trade by the early 1570s. Actually, this was before England had much of an influence in Africa or the Americas, so he would often "steal" slaves from Portuguese or Spanish traders in Africa and then sell them to the other side of the Americas. While he was doing this, he also had time to engage in plenty of other piratical activities, which eventually gained him the official status of privateer by Queen Elizabeth I of England.

The status may have given Drake an air of legitimacy, but it didn't stop him from robbing and killing throughout the Americas and Europe. By all accounts, Drake was a very nasty dude, which is precisely what Elizabeth thought she needed in her quest to create a British empire.

On December 15, 1577, Drake and 163 other sailors left England in five ships on a voyage of "discovery" to the New World. The fact that the voyage was called this title is quite absurd on the face of it because the primary intention was for Drake and his small fleet to disrupt Spanish shipping in the Caribbean.

The expedition went reasonably well for Drake at first, as they captured plenty of Spanish ships and gold, but by the time they reached what is today Argentina, things weren't looking so good. There was talk of mutiny and Drake was quickly losing control of his men, so he decided to make an example.

Although he had no real evidence, Drake charged Thomas Doughty, one of his high-ranking crew members, with treason and witchcraft.

As absurd as the charges against Doughty were, the trial was a kangaroo court of unmitigated proportions. Drake lied that he had royal sanction to convene the trial and then went on to convict the hapless sailor, sentence him to death, and behead him for the entire crew to see.

Drake then led his men through the Strait of Magellan and raided Spanish colonies on the Pacific coast in South and North America. Drake made friends with some of the natives he met, killed others, but always made sure to take anything of value with him before moving on to the next country.

Francis Drake finally returned to England on September 26, 1580, an immensely famous and rich man.

Truly, Francis Drake has a complex and somewhat bizarre personal history that some would call absurd, while others would say it's phenomenal.

On the one hand, no one can deny that Drake was a thief, killer, and scoundrel, but on the other hand, he was a brave explorer who opened the world to new possibilities, proving that sometimes beneath the absurd is greatness waiting to get out.

The Many Loves of Ramesses the Great

The great crooner Frank Sinatra once sang that love and marriage went together "like a horse and carriage." Although I'm not quite sure if that's such a ringing endorsement of the institution, it does seem to fit in many ways. It takes plenty of time and commitment to make a marriage work because the alternative is divorce, which is usually economically and psychologically draining.

Of course, there are the privileged few who can seemingly wed serially without repercussions. A recent example is actress Liz Taylor, who married seven times before she died, and death was probably the only thing that stopped her from marrying again.

But as absurd as Liz Taylor's "commitment" to the institution of marriage was, there are even more absurd, crazier cases from the annals of world history.

One of the best cases of a person who loved, and loved again, and again, was the ancient Egyptian pharaoh, Ramesses II (ruled c. 1279-1213 BCE), better known as Ramesses "the Great."

Ramesses is best remembered for being quite boastful and hyperbolic in the texts where he describes his involvement in a battle at a place called Kadesh (aka Qadesh) in what is today Syria. The great king is even better known for being quite prolific in his commissioning of temples and monuments that still bear his name and can be seen throughout Egypt.

But Ramesses was prolific in other things as well.

He was a guy that definitely loved women, but unlike Liz Taylor or any other notable celebrity, he didn't have to divorce his wives when he got tired of them…he just added the new ones to his harem.

Polygamy, the idea of plural marriage, was a not-so-uncommon institution in the pre-modern world, especially ancient Egypt, but Ramesses took the idea to entirely new and absurd levels. Ramesses is recorded as having seven "Royal Wives," which may not seem like much, especially when you consider they weren't all his wives at the same time, but the number grows when his "lesser wives" and concubines are considered.

Modern scholars know about Ramesses' favorite wife, Nefertari, and the woman who replaced her, Isetnofret, but the precise numbers become a bit fuzzy in the later part of the king's reign.

Since Ramesses ruled nearly 67 years and lived to be around 100, the records are sometimes confusing as to which wives lived at the same time. In total, Ramesses probably had at least 100 wives and concubines and as many as several hundred, which is certainly absurd and difficult to comprehend.

Did he really see all of his wives and mistresses regularly? And if so, how was he able to have the energy, especially at his advanced age?

I guess we'll probably never know the answer to those questions, no matter how hard we look.

But as strange as that may be, the most absurd, but real, fact about Ramesses the Great's many loves was that four of his wives were also his daughters!

Consanguineous marriage is illegal in most countries today, and contrary to common belief, it wasn't popular in ancient Egypt until later. But Ramesses the Great was so full of himself that he thought marrying some of his daughters would be the best way to keep his bloodlines pure. He married Bintanath, a daughter he had with Isetnofret, and Meryatum, whom he had with Nefertari, during his long life. He actually ended up marrying four of his daughters to keep his bloodline pure.

I know that sensibilities change throughout time and across cultures, but I think most people today would agree that Ramesses the Great's love life was pretty wild and totally absurd.

13

I Never Would've Thought of Putting Dead Dogs on Saddles

History is full of some pretty violent, outrageous tyrants who've done some pretty absurd things. In modern times, there's the example of Mao Zedong attempting to kill all the sparrows in China and Muammar Gaddafi's extremely eccentric behavior in Libya.

But long before either of these two came to power, the brutal ruler Ivan IV, better known today as Ivan "the Terrible," ruled Russia with an iron fist from 1547 to 1584. Initially known as the Grand Prince of Moscow 1533-1547, he was crowned Tsar of Russia from 1547 - until his death in 1584.

Ivan was the first Russian ruler to be crowned "Tsar of all Russia," and for the first 15 years or so, things went well for the most part. Russia was expanding into the east and south and there was more or less domestic tranquility on the home front - most of the population was living in serfdom, but they had for centuries, and they were not rebellious. So, all was good for Ivan.

But then Russia suffered setbacks in the Livonian War and in 1564, Ivan moved from the capital of Moscow to the small town of Aleksandrova, about 60 miles away. Historians are still in disagreement over whether this was the beginning of a mental breakdown for Ivan, or if it was a carefully thought-out plan.

Whatever the case, after a few months, Ivan returned to Moscow in February 1565, rejuvenated and ready to go to work. Ivan's work wasn't what most leaders tend to do, though. Instead of having some bridges built or signing some diplomatic agreements, Ivan decided to go to war against the *boyars*, or nobles.

Ivan immediately announced he was enacting a policy known as the *oprichnina*, which is a Russian word that roughly translates into "apart" or "beside." Whether due to irrational paranoia or legitimate fear, Ivan hated the boyars, so the oprichnina program was meant to kill, dispossess, or exile a vast majority of the Russian nobles.

But to carry out such an ambitious plan, Ivan needed manpower, which is where this story begins veering into the absurd.

Ivan handpicked a force of men that numbered 1,000 to 6,000, known as the *Oprichniki*, to carry out his orders. The Oprichniki wore all black, rode black horses, and perhaps most absurd, and a bit scary, each one had a dog's head tied to his saddle.

But as silly as riding around with a dog's head on a saddle may seem, you wouldn't have been laughing if you were a noble and the Oprichniki showed up at your estate. Chances are, the Oprichniki would've had their way with your wife before killing you and burning your property to the ground.

The Oprichniki killed thousands of Russian nobles from 1565 to 1572, often with Ivan riding along with them, watching as they committed atrocity after atrocity.

Some historians believe that Ivan's second wife, Maria, actually mitigated the Oprichnina to a large extent, pleading with Ivan to spare the lives of many of the nobles by exiling them instead. When the beautiful Maria died in 1569 at the tender age of 25, it possibly sent the already mentally unstable Ivan over the edge.

Ivan's war against the nobles ramped up; then, without notice and little attention, Ivan unceremoniously abolished the Oprichnina in 1575. His absurd behavior grew worse, though. The peak came in 1581 when he beat his pregnant daughter-in-law for her immodest dress and then stabbed his own son to death when he attempted to intervene.

Riding around with dog heads on your saddle may seem very absurd, and it was no doubt smelly, but in Ivan the Terrible's case, it was just one of many signs of just how unhinged the Tsar really was.

Did Chastity Belts Really Work?

We've seen how the ideas surrounding love, marriage, and sex have remained the same in some ways throughout history but have also changed in some notable instances. Sex work, the oldest profession in the world, was institutionalized in ancient Mesopotamia, and polygamy, which is outlawed in most places today, was common among royalty in the ancient world.

Then there's the idea of celibacy and chastity.

You'd be naïve to think that people weren't having sex before marriage before World War II (as a typical marker of when the world's attitudes toward sex generally changed). It certainly happened, and although there were some birth control methods before the pill, some better than others, "whoops" pregnancies were not uncommon. In most of those cases, the young man and the young woman married, and all the problems were solved.

But things could get complicated for married couples, especially when the husband was away for extended periods.

In the pre-modern world, it was important for a man to know that his wife was faithful and that if she had a child, he was certain it was his.

Remember, this was long before DNA tests or Maury Povich. It was also centuries before the feminist movement, so women pretty much had to go along with this system.

So, during the Middle Ages, when the husband was away fighting in the Crusades or some other war for an extended period, he needed to know his wife was faithful and not giving birth to another man's children. For years, it was believed the common answer to this was the chastity belt.

The chastity belt, as described in a few historical documents, and in the even fewer examples that still exist, was simply a girdle that covered the woman's vagina enough to prevent penetration but not enough to stop urination. Some chastity belts were believed to be a bit more ornate, complicated, and dangerous.

One example, a chastity belt said to have been from the ruler of Venice's palace in the 1500s or 1600s is a bit scary looking, to say the least. It looks like a standard chastity belt except for pieces that cover the wearer's vagina, and the anus being open - but with plenty of spikes!

That would certainly make someone think twice before doing the deed, that's for sure!

But as strange as the concept of chastity belts were, the questions remain: did they work, and were they even widely used?

The answer to the first question is yes, to a certain degree. A chastity belt would've been difficult to put on a person, and to take off, so the likelihood of a lonely lady in the castle cutting one off for a quick dalliance was unlikely, but if she had a very determined paramour...

But the more important question here is, were they even widely used, and the answer to that appears to be mixed.

There is very little evidence that chastity belts were used in the Middle Ages, as commonly believed. Chastity belts don't appear to have been used much until the 1500s, and even then, they were limited. This may be a myth and legend created after the event?

Who has the time to build such a contraption in the first place, right? And even though women had much less of a say in things back then than they do today, you can't tell me noblewomen, who came from families with money and influence, would so easily go along with it.

The most absurd thing about chastity belts is that, by the late 1800s, people were using them as anti-masturbation devices, and more recently they've been utilized as toys in kinky sex games.

But as weird as all that may seem, maybe it's just a case of people trying to inhibit, and then promote, the biological drive to have sex. Most people are fine doing things without a belt, spikes or otherwise!

No TV for You!

Like it or not, television is a part of modern society that doesn't show any signs of going away. Even with the rise of the computer and the internet, television has adapted in the form of digital sets and smart TVs, which allow average sets to access the internet and streaming services. We may disparage the influence TV has on our society, call it the "boob tube," and try to limit our consumption of it, but the reality is that there's probably one in your home right now.

There are multiple sets in my home!

And for those you over the age of 40, it was a major part of your life. TV programs were must-see before the 2000s, where you had to watch your favorite shows on time (well, there was the videotape thing, but that's another story), and families and friends would routinely gather to watch special events. And back in those days, if kids were naughty, the punishment was often loss of TV privileges.

So, with all of that in mind, it would seem pretty absurd that a country didn't have TV well into the 1970s, right? I mean, where did that happen, and better yet, *how* could that happen?

Well, when the technology of television began making its way around the world after World War II, the Republic of South Africa was a unique place, to say the least. The government was ruled by the White minority under what was known as the apartheid system, but within the Black and White population, several different ethnic groups spoke just as many languages.

So, the government's ruling National Party, which was pro-apartheid and pro-Afrikaner (a primarily Dutch descended ethnic group), perceived TV as a threat to their power. They believed that if they allowed TV into their country, English language shows that promoted racial equality would be a bad influence on the population.

They also saw TV as a difficult business proposition because of the many different languages spoken in South Africa.

So, the government gave a hard pass on TV.

But after a while, many in the government, even hardliners, began to think they were taking an absurd stance against the "little black box." South Africans were missing out on some pretty big things, such as the World Cup, the Olympics, rugby, and the Moon landing, so they argued it was time to change.

But in countries like South Africa, change is slow, and it wouldn't be until 1976 that television was first allowed.

You can argue that South Africa was or wasn't better off without television, but there's no arguing the fact that the country's long-time ban on technology is truly strange and almost inconceivable to most people today.

From Sex Worker to Empress

Few women have influenced the course of European history more than Theodora, the wife of Byzantine Emperor Justinian I (ruled 527-548 CE). Historians have recognized Theodora for her sharp mind and cunning political abilities, while the Greek and many other Orthodox Christian churches have venerated the 6th-century empress as a saint.

But her "professional" origins were anything but saintly.

Theodora was born into a commoner family around the year 500 in either Cyprus or Syria. Her father was initially a bear trainer for the Hippodrome in Constantinople and upon his death, her mother brought her children wearing garlands into the hippodrome and presented them as suppliants to the Blue Faction chariot racing team. From then on, Theodora would be their supporter and her family became heavily involved with the Blue team.

Chariot racing was a rough and tough world in the Byzantine Empire, about the furthest one can be from the nobility, which makes Theodora's ascent pretty incredible.

Theodora grew up around the hooligan violence that often happened between the supporters of the different chariot racing teams, and when she became old enough, she went into acting.

Although the people of Byzantium loved drama, the acting profession was considered rather unsavory, to say the least (some things don't change!), as actresses also often doubled as sex workers. Theodora worked as a sex worker for many years before she became a wealthy man's mistress, but he dumped her in North Africa, alone and broke.

Theodora ended up in Alexandria, Egypt, where she had a religious epiphany and became an ardent follower of the Coptic Orthodox Church. The details of what happened next and how she met the future emperor are a bit murky.

She definitely kept her old contacts with the Blues, but it isn't certain if she went back into sex work. But however it happened, she met Justinian in 524 CE and immediately enchanted the young noble.

The fact that Theodora wasn't of noble birth was one thing, but that she was an "actress" was what really prevented Justinian from marrying her at first. But true love is a tough thing to stop, especially when it involves someone as powerful as Justinian. The emperor Justin I passed a law that allowed his adopted son, Justinian, to marry Theodora, making the real-life, medieval version of *Pretty Woman* a reality.

And once Theodora became empresses, she was no shrinking violet. She played a key role in many of her husband's political and diplomatic victories, as well as a couple of defeats, and even opposed him on important religious issues.

Theodora's ascent from being a lowly sex worker to the most powerful woman proves that sometimes even the most absurd and seemingly unbelievable things really can become reality.

Strange but True History Facts

- Of the 164 men and boys who departed with Drake from England, only 58 returned.

- Another absurd fact about Ivan IV is his nickname. His nickname, *Grozny*, has often been translated into English as "Terrible," but most scholars think, "formidable or sparking terror or fear" is a closer translation.

- Sex work was for the most part legal and widespread in the United States until the late 1800s. Brothels were common in the big cities in the east and in the smaller frontier towns of the west, casinos and bars doubled as brothels (yes, "saloon girls" were sex workers). This all began coming to an end when the federal government started to crack down on brothels in the early 1900s.

- It's pretty ironic that ten years after the apartheid government in South Africa first allowed television, the most popular show among the White population was *The Cosby Show*.

- As stated earlier, incestuous/consanguineous marriage was uncommon in ancient Egypt, although Ramesses the Great apparently tried to make it so. After Alexander the Great conquered Egypt and the Greek "Ptolemy" Dynasty was installed there in 305 BCE, consanguineous marriage, particularly between brother and sister, was all but institutionalized. Modern Egyptologists believe part of the reason why this absurd form of marriage became so popular for the Ptolemies was that they didn't properly understand the Egyptian language. The ancient Egyptians usually referred to each other as "brother" and "sister", even husbands and wives, so the Ptolemies, who only knew Greek, may have misunderstood this.

- The proper name for Theodora's occupation before she was an empress was "courtesan." In many pre-modern societies, courtesans were well-educated women who were knowledgeable in a range of subjects, including sex.

- South Africa was not the last country on the African continent to bring TV to its people; that absurd honor would go to Tanzania, which didn't first allow TV until the 1990s.

- Ramesses the Great who ruled for 67 years, may not have been the only centenarian to sit on the Egyptian throne. Pepi I (ruled c. 2321-2287 BCE) reigned in the Sixth Dynasty in the Old Kingdom for about 40 years. Also known as Pepy I. Although Pepi may have lived as long as Ramesses, he does not appear to have been as lucky in love, *only* having six known wives.

- There are several legends about Drake's "lost treasures" stashed around the world, but so far none have been found.

- The world's shortest war is thought to be the Anglo-Zanzibar War; it only took 38 - 45 minutes for the British to defeat Zanzibar on August 27, 1896.

CHAPTER 2:

WAY OUT POP CULTURE AND SPORTS

We now move from bizarre history into some truly baffling but true stories from sports and pop culture. We'll take a look at everything from pretty absurd sports rules to some seemingly unbelievable sports events.

When we're not looking at some of the strangest moments in sports history, we'll examine some absurd events connected to celebrities. I know more than a few of you reading this are thinking, "Aren't celebrities and the word 'absurd' redundant?" Well, I can't honestly argue with you on that one, although this chapter will introduce you to a few true head-scratchers. And more than one true mystery.

So, keep reading to find out just how absurd the often already bizarre worlds of pop culture and sports can really get!

Who Knew Strychnine and Brandy Were Performance Enhancing Drugs?

The original Olympic games began in 776BC in Greece and ended in 393AD. Since they were so long ago, they were certainly far different than the Olympics today in the number and type of events held, the rules pertaining to them, and who was allowed to participate. The original Olympics were a purely Greek-speaking affair and for men only: there were no ancient equivalents of Nadia Comaneci or Mary Lou Retton.

For centuries, the memories of the Olympics could only be found in history books, until some wealthy and influential Europeans got together to restart a modern version of the games on April 6, 1896.

In many ways, the original version of the new games was very much like the old version. It was limited to men until 1900, and women were only allowed in limited events, and apart from the Americans, South Africans, and Australians, it was a European affair. Of course, that's all changed in the decades since, but there was one other notable, and absurd, element the early, modern Olympics shared with the ancient games -a lack of regulation.

The 1904 Summer Olympics took place in St. Louis, Missouri, with the Midwest city hoping to impress visiting Europeans with its combination of middle American industriousness and Mississippi River charm.

It was a bit of a toned-down affair, with only 15 nations competing, but St. Louis did its best to represent and hoped that the marathon would be the highlight of the games.

Almost immediately, though, things went wrong.

The first problem was the officials began the race at 3 p.m. on August 30. St. Louis is known for being warm and muggy, and on that day, it was about 90°F and humid when the race started.

Three hours and 13 minutes after the race began, American Fred Lorz came across the finish line to the cheers of the crowd. But before Lorz could be awarded the gold medal, it was learned that he actually dropped out of the race after nine miles with cramps, hitched a ride in a car for ten miles, and then ran the final 4.85 miles to the finish!

Lorz tried to play it off as a joke, but the Amateur Athletic Union didn't think it was too funny, giving him a lifetime ban that was later reduced to a year.

About 15 minutes after the not-so-surprisingly fresh Lorz trotted across the finish line, American Thomas Hicks came in at a time of three hours and 28 minutes. Hicks' win was legitimate *for the era*, but there's no way it would be allowed today.

Actually, the tactics he used wouldn't be considered by even the most unscrupulous athletes.

As Hicks struggled in the day's heat, which was exacerbated by a lack of water stations along the route, his commanding lead was in danger of evaporating when he nearly passed out on several occasions. So, his trainers did what any good trainers at the time would do: they gave him a shot of brandy mixed with a little strychnine.

Yes, you read that correctly! Hick's trainers gave him *rat poison* to push him across the finish line!

As weird as it may sound, strychnine can stimulate the nervous system and in Hick's case, it worked because it did apparently give him a bit of a boost that allowed him to take the gold.

The unconventional performance-enhancing drugs Thomas Hicks took in the 1904 Summer Olympics was just the most absurd part of a race that, by the time it finally ended, was replete with several unexpected turns of events. You could certainly make a case for it being the craziest, most bizarre sports event in history.

Paul McCartney's Double

Conspiracy theories are quite common in the world of politics and big business. The shady dealings of government leaders, CEOs, and other men and women who hold levers of power are often thought to be even shadier than they are and controlled by people behind the scenes. But since conspiracy theories often neatly explain inexplicable things, and because they're fun, they've also managed to make their way into other areas of life, including pop culture.

Did you know that Paul McCartney, the bass player and leading vocalist of the legendary rock band the Beatles died in a car crash on November 9, 1966, and was replaced with a double?

Well, that didn't really happen - or at least I don't *think* it did - but it's one of the most absurd conspiracy theories in pop culture history, or all history, for that matter. According to the theory, Paul left a recording session on the night in question, angry at his bandmates. After they became successful, The Beatles often feuded, with drugs and alcohol usually in the mix. The angry McCartney lost control of his car and was killed in a single-car accident.

Then the story starts to get absurd.

Instead of announcing to the world that Paul McCartney was dead, the Beatles, through their manager Brian Epstein, found a guy who looked enough like him and was presumably musically talented, to fill the role. Various theories link British intelligence agency MI5 to the conspiracy and/or the American CIA.

There were murmurs that Paul had died and been replaced, but they remained murmurs on the fringes of society until the student newspaper of Drake University in Des Moines, Iowa, the *Drake Times-Delphic*, published an article on September 17, 1969, questioning the musician's death. The article was followed up in October of that year by Detroit radio DJ, Russ Gibb, who discussed the "evidence" of Paul's death live on the air.

The evidence in question came from several "clues" from Beatles albums. The 1967 album, *Sgt. Pepper's Lonely Hearts Club Band*, included a back-masked line on the song "Revolution 9", which when played backwards *possibly* sounds like it says "Turn me on, dead man."

Then, on the 1968 *White Album*, another clue was seemingly revealed when lead vocalist John Lennon proclaimed, "The Walrus was Paul." The reference was to the song "I Am the Walrus" from the Beatle's 1967 *Magical Mystery Tour* album. Who or what exactly the walrus was, remains a mystery, though?

Perhaps the greatest "clue" to this mystery, if it even is a mystery, is on the cover of the Beatles 1969 *Abbey Road* album. On the cover, Beatles members John Lennon, George Harrison, and Ringo Starr are each walking across a crosswalk with their left foot forward, while McCartney conspicuously is walking with his right foot forward, and barefooted.

But as strange as the anecdotal evidence may be, the obvious question is, why would anyone go to such lengths to cover up what was - in all versions of the story - an accident?

Well, one claim is that the other members of the band, and Epstein, didn't want the gravy train to end, so they hired a stand-in from a Beatles look-a-like contest.

Another theory, which is a bit more absurd but also more fun, states that the Beatles were a Western intelligence operation designed to infiltrate and control the counterculture. The CIA *was* documented as infiltrating the counterculture in the 1960s but replacing him with a double seems pretty far-fetched.

For his part, McCartney gave an interview in late October 1969 from his farm in Scotland, dispelling the rumors.

But not everyone was convinced he was the real Paul McCartney, especially since he had grown some stubble and didn't look like the Paul his fans were used to seeing.

Life on the farm has a way of doing that to a person!

Eventually, the absurdity of the idea that Paul McCartney had died and been replaced began to subside, but you only have to do a simple web search to find there are still people of people who believe it was "Raul," not Paul, who went on to have a successful career after the Beatles with Wings and as a solo artist in the 1970s and '80s.

An Absurdly Deadly Film

From the strange conspiracy theory of Paul McCartney's double, let's move on to the scary urban legend about the lethal film *Atuk*. Actually, *Atuk* was never completed because every actor who got the lead part died, which is enough for this legend to make our list.

The story of Atuk began in 1963 when the novel *The Incomparable Atuk* by Mordecai Richler was first published. The plot features an Inuit man named Atuk who travels from the territory of Nunavut, Canada to Toronto, Ontario, finding that life in the big city is quite different.

Although the book sold well, it was quickly relegated to the quirky shelves of equally quirky bookstores, where it remained until some film producers and writers got a hold of it.

Director Norman Jewison liked the fish-out-of-water idea of the book, but he thought some major changes were in order. He hired writer Tod Carroll to write the script, making Atuk half Inuit (there were no Inuit actors to speak of that time and very few American Indian actors, for that matter), overweight, and from Alaska instead of Canada. Additionally, the film would be set in New York instead of Toronto and would focus on the lighthearted aspects of cultural misunderstandings, just as *Crocodile Dundee* would later do.

So, the search for the actor who'd play Atuk began and quickly ended with John Belushi. Belushi was at the top of his game in the early 1980s, being one of the primary cast members of *Saturday Night Live* and starring in box office hits such as *Animal House.*

But tragedy struck when Belushi died from a cocaine-heroin overdose -known as a "speedball" - on March 5, 1982.

The film was over before filming began, but the idea and script were still seen as having potential, so film company United

Artists bought the rights to it and began looking for the next Atuk in 1988.

The role went to comedian and actor Sam Kinison that year, who was peaking in popularity with his bawdy brand of humor. But like Belushi, Kinison suffered from substance abuse problems and was difficult to work with. Production on the film stopped but then restarted in 1992.

Then tragedy struck once more when Kinison was killed in a head-on collision by a drunk driver on April 10, 1992, at the age of 38.

The *Atuk* script was eventually handed off to screenwriter Michael O'Donoghue, who is rumored to have suggested the ebullient actor John Candy for the title role.

Although John Candy was known for his family-friendly roles, like Belushi and Kinison, he struggled with demons that included overeating, alcoholism, and drug abuse. Not long after he first read the *Atuk* script, John Candy died on March 4, 1994, at the age of 43 from a heart attack.

Then O'Donoghue died on November 8, 1994.

As the bodies involved with *Atuk* started piling up before a second of the movie was even filmed, more than a few people began to take notice, but it wasn't enough for the execs at United Artists to stop production.

So, United went back to the drawing board and approached Chris Farley for the role in 1996.

If you're not familiar with Farley, his style of comedic acting was sort of a mix of John Belushi and John Candy. He had the bulky build and overall similar look of Candy but with the frenetic and unpredictable nature of Belushi, with a little Sam Kinison thrown in for good measure. He seemed like the perfect actor to play Atuk, and his friend and fellow *Saturday Night Live* alum, Phil Hartman, was positioned to take a role in the film as a straight man.

Well, Farley, much like Belushi, died of a speedball overdose on December 18, 1997, at the age of 33, which was also Belushi's age when he died.

And as a macabre postscript to this story, Hartman was murdered by his wife on May 27, 1998.

I don't know if *Atuk* has been cursed for some reason, or even if curses exist, but I do know that circumstances surrounding its production are beyond weird and definitely more than a little bit scary. It'll be interesting to see if another film company *attempts* to make the movie…or if any actors will accept the leading role.

The One-Handed Pitcher Who Threw a No-Hitter

If you weren't a fan of Major League Baseball during the 1990s and you happen to take a look at retired pitcher Jim Abbott's stat line, it doesn't necessarily jump out as all that impressive. From 1989 until he retired after the 1999 season, Abbott compiled an 87-108 record with a 4.25 ERA.

Abbott did have a couple of notable bright spots during his career. He won 18 games with the California Angels in 1991 and pitched a no-hitter with the New York Yankees in 1993. So, not bad statistics, but nothing earth-shattering. The truth is, by most measures, Jim Abbott should've never started even in a little league game, never mind the Majors because he was born without his right hand!

Jim Abbott's no-hitter against the Cleveland Indians on September 4, 1993, was the apex of a career that many see as absurdly phenomenal, but I see it as wildly inspirational.

Despite being born without a right hand, Abbott was gifted with natural athletic abilities, had an excellent work ethic, and was blessed with a great family. It also didn't hurt that Abbott was a lefty and lefty pitchers are also a highly prized commodity.

Still, the odds were against Abbott even making his high school team, so he had to develop a method whereby he could hold a glove and field with only one hand. And this is where Abbott's abilities truly proved to be absurd in the most positive and inspiring way.

Abbott would keep his glove on the end of his right arm while he threw a pitch, and as soon as he did, he would nearly instantaneously switch the glove to his left hand.

The move worked so well that he was able to blow through the competition while he was in high school and college in Michigan. Abbott went on the pitch for the US baseball team in the 1988 Summer Olympics, where he became the first pitcher in 25 years to beat the seemingly unbeatable Cuban national team. He then went on to defeat Japan in the gold medal game.

Abbott's amateur success translated into him being drafted as the eighth pick of the first round in the amateur baseball draft by the California Angels. Due to his success at the University of Michigan and on the Olympic team, Abbott bypassed the minors for the majors.

As soon as he made his first start in the majors, Abbott amazed fans with his natural pitching talent and his ability to switch glove hands. By the time Abbot pitched his no-hitter in 1993, he was already a bit of a legend and a favorite on the sports highlight reels.

Today, people who've never heard of Jim Abbott may think the idea of a pitcher with only one hand even coming close to playing in the Major Leagues is absurd, but Abbott proved that sometimes the only absurdities in life are the limits we place on ourselves.

Celebrity Doppelgangers

You've probably heard the saying that everyone has a double or a doppelganger. Maybe you've met someone who looks so much like you they could be your brother or sister, or maybe you've noticed the doppelganger phenomenon among other people, such as celebrities.

And make no mistake about it, when you take a closer look, it's a bit eerie how many celebrities, past and present, really do have a doppelganger often working in the same industry as them, and sometimes even on the same films!

The reason for the phenomenon may be as simple as typecasting, as film and TV producers look for a certain "type" that is more common in Hollywood and among the "beautiful people."

Or maybe there's something more supernatural at work that brings these people together? That may seem absurd, but as we've seen already in this book, sometimes absurdity is the rule not the exception in life. Let's take a look at a few of my favorite celebrity doppelgangers so you can be the judge.

Actor Zooey Deschanel and singer Katy Perry look so much alike that they should be at the top of any celebrity double list, but I think a close second is a British actress Keira Knightley and American actress Natalie Portman. The two women are of similar age and height, and most importantly, they have remarkably similar facial features, so much so that Knightley played the role of Portman's character's double in *Star Wars: Episode I – The Phantom Menace.*

Another celebrity pairing that looks amazingly like they are brothers from another mother is actors Liam Neeson and Ralph Fiennes. The two men are friends and noticeably starred opposite each other in the 1994 film *Schindler's List.*

Other notable celebrity doppelgangers who you may have recently noticed include Zoe Saldana and Thandie Newton, Michael Cera and Jesse Eisenberg, and Gerard Butler and Clive Owen.

Some of my favorite celebrity doppelgangers are those a little less known and those no longer with us.

If you've watched enough detective shows from the 1970s or any TV show or movie that had a biker in a bit part, then you certainly saw either Dennis Burkley or Mickey Jones a time or two. Both men were known for their bulky physiques and bearded faces and were also commonly mistaken for each other.

If a doppelganger is a double, then I guess a trio of celebrity look-a-likes would be a tripleganger, or a trioganger? Whatever you want to call it, George Hamilton, Fernando Lamas, and George Maharis all seemed to look eerily alike when they were at their peaks in the late 1960s and 1970s. All three men epitomized the "tall, dark, and handsome" look that was popular on the small and big screens during that era.

I've just scratched the surface of this strange subject. I'm sure if you sit down and think about it, especially with some friends, you can come up with some other interesting celebrity doppelgangers from the past and present.

Disaster Drafts

We often think of professional athletes as being almost a species apart from the rest of us. Besides the adulation many people give them, and the exorbitant salaries they are often paid, the fact that they are in a state of physical fitness no average person could ever hope to achieve certainly puts them a rung above the rest of us, at least physically.

But no matter how physically fit professional athletes may be, there's little they can do when the grim reaper comes calling. Several professional athletes have died in accidents, and a few have been murdered while in their primes, which sometimes hurt their teams. Since professional sports teams are often put together to be almost like a finely-tuned machine, where the slightest problems can ruin a team's season, the permanent loss of a star player could destroy a team's success for years.

But what would happen if all or nearly all players on a team were to suddenly die?

As absurd as the question may seem, it has happened.

The most notable examples are when the 1970 Marshal University football team's plane crashed, killing most of the players and coaches, and a plane crash in 1977 that killed the Evansville University men's basketball team. Other notable team disasters include a 1956 plane crash that killed five members of two different Canadian Football League teams, a 1979 mid-air collision that killed all the members of a professional Uzbek soccer team, and a 1936 train crash in Italy that killed the coach and left all the players of the L'Aquila Calcio soccer team unable to continue their playing careers.

So, a disaster that could wipe an entire team out may seem absurd, and the odds of it happening are absurdly remote, but it's not out of the realm of possibility.

And if it did happen in professional sports, it could ruin the season of not just the team directly affected, but the entire league. If you're a sports fan and you followed sports in 2020 then you noticed how much Covid-19 disrupted the schedules and the amount of money it cost the leagues and teams. Now imagine what would happen if one of a particular league's teams suddenly wasn't there at all.

The owners of Major League Baseball (MLB), the National Basketball Association (NBA), the National Football League (NFL), the National Hockey League, Major League Soccer (MLS), and the Russian Kontinental Hockey League (KHL) all have a provision to deal with such a tragedy, which is commonly known as a "disaster draft."

The details of the disaster draft vary in the different leagues, but it essentially works as a special draft if one of the teams in a league were to lose a set number of players to a tragedy. The team affected would be allowed to draft a certain number of players from the other teams, while the other teams in the league are allowed to "protect" a minimum number of players.

The disaster draft may seem strange, and a bit absurd, but it's totally real. Hopefully, though, a disaster draft will never have to be held.

The Bizarre Murder Case of Karyn Kupcinet

When the Los Angeles newspapers and TV stations reported on the murder of a young actress named Karyn Kupcinet, few people paid attention. Any other time the murder of a young, beautiful actress would have garnered plenty of attention, but this was November 28, 1963, which just so happened to be six days after President John F. Kennedy was assassinated.

The country had bigger things to worry about than the murder of an up-and-coming actress, but the local police did investigate Kupcinet's murder, and the result was one of the most absurd and bizarre murder cases in Hollywood's history. And that's saying a lot when you think about all the other examples.

There's the mysterious 1959 death of actor George Reeves and the equally mysterious death of Natalie Wood in 1981.

And who can forget the murder of Nicole Brown Simpson in 1994 or the unsolved murder of rapper Tupac Shakur in 1996?

But the Karyn Kupcinet murder is much stranger due to its circumstances and the fact that there were plenty of suspects but never any arrests.

Kupcinet was born Roberta Kupcinet in 1941 in Chicago, Illinois to newspaper writer Irv Kupcinet and his wife Esther.

Thanks to her father's connections in the media industry, Roberta was able to land some small TV roles in the early 1960s and make a move to Hollywood. She took the screen name of Karyn (I can't say I blame her as I can't recall any big-name actresses named Roberta) and immediately fell into the Hollywood lifestyle. Kupcinet had a small house in West Hollywood and began dating her young up-and-coming actor neighbor, Andrew Prine.

But on the evening of November 28, everything came to a sudden and mysterious end for the actress.

Kupcinet visited the home of her friends, Mark and Marcia Goddard (in case you're wondering, yes, it was *that* Mark Goddard who later starred on *Lost in Space*), on that evening for dinner. The Goddard's said Kupcinet ate very little and was acting strangely, indicating that she was potentially under the influence of drugs.

Kupcinet then left the Goddard home and returned to her own home where she was joined by two friends, Edward Rubin and Robert Hathaway. The two men claimed that Kupcinet eventually fell asleep on the couch and later retired to her bedroom. They then left and met up with Prine, who was also their friend, and they spent the rest of the night with him.

The Goddard's were a bit disturbed by their visit with Kupcinet, so when they didn't hear back from her, Mark went to her home to check on her. He found her naked and dead on the couch.

An autopsy was performed on Kupcinet's body, revealing that she died of a broken hyoid bone and that she was likely strangled to death.

Here's where this story begins to get absurd and bizarre.

Since he was Kupcinet's boyfriend, and he admitted they had been quarreling, Prine was the prime suspect from the start. Rubin and Hathaway were also high on the suspect list because they were the last people who claimed to have seen Kupcinet alive.

No arrests were ever made, and life went on for everyone involved. Prine continued to act, but he was relegated to guest-starring roles on TV shows and leading roles in B films and exploitation flicks, such as *Simon, King of Witches*.

But as the years went by, a new theory about Karyn Kupcinet's murder began circulating - it was meant as a warning to her father from people involved in the Kennedy assassination.

The theory is that Irv Kupcinet was involved with the mafia and that he, and Karyn, somehow received advanced notice of the assassination.

There isn't much evidence to support mafia involvement in Kupcinet's murder, other than the Kupcinet family was from Chicago and may have rubbed shoulders with some wise guys over the years; but a well-planned assassination wouldn't leave many trails, right?

Many people think that it's absurd to even consider Karyn Kupcinet's murder along with the Kennedy assassination, but if there's one thing you should've learned from this book by now, it's that the absurd is more common than we think.

Absurd Sports Rules

The world of sports is full of many strange rules, and it seems the older the sport, the stranger the rules. We already took a look at the absurdly macabre disaster draft rule that some professional sports leagues have in place in "The One-Handed Pitcher Who Threw a No-Hitter", now let's look at a litany of other obscure rules from around the world.

Football leagues around the world - that includes American and Canadian football, rugby, soccer, and Australian and Gaelic football - all have very strict rules about how many players can be on the field at a time. Violations of the rule can result in lost yards or penalty kicks, but in Australian rules football, it can cost a team the game in one sweep.

According to the Australian football rulebook, if a team that has too many players on the field is caught, they lose all of the points they've scored until that point in the game. Now that's harsh!

Soccer/Football is a sport where apart from the goalkeeper, hands are strictly verboten. So, have you ever watched a game and noticed that sometimes when a keeper is holding the ball, they start dribbling like a basketball? Well, that's due to one of the stranger rules of soccer.

According to the International Federation of Football (FIFA) rulebook, the goalkeeper is the only player allowed to hold the ball, but they can only do so for six seconds, after which they must release it from their hands. Most keepers kick the ball away or throw it to a team member, but occasionally you'll see some bouncing going on, which is totally acceptable under the rules.

My favorite absurd sports rule is Major League Baseball's "Pat Venditte Rule." The eponymously named rule went into effect in 2008 that limited an ambidextrous (yes, he could pitch left *and* right) pitcher's ability to take advantage of his unique gift. According to the rule, any ambidextrous pitcher must announce to the umpire and batter before the at-bat which hand they are pitching from, and they must continue pitching with that hand until the end of the at-bat.

Needless to say, the Pat Venditte Rule hasn't seen much use since Venditte left the game in 2020.

Strange but True Pop Culture and Sports Facts

- Cuban mailman Andarin Carvajal traveled to the United States to compete in the 1904 Summer Olympic marathon but almost didn't make it. He lost all his money gambling in New Orleans, then had to hitchhike to St. Louis, ate some wild apples that made him sick, and ultimately ran in his street clothes. Despite the setbacks, Carvajal just missed out on medaling, finishing fourth!

- David Furr was the only member of the Evansville basketball team who wasn't on the doomed flight. He was at home nursing an ankle injury when his teammates all died. But apparently, it really was Furr's time to go because about two weeks later he died in a car accident.

- Since Jim Abbott spent most of his career in the American League, he didn't have to worry about hitting, although he did have a maneuver for that as well. He would bat left, so his good hand held the upper portion of the bat and provided most of the motion.

- The murder of American publicist Ronni Chasen is another significant unsolved celebrity murder. Chasen was shot to death on November 16, 2010, in Beverly Hills as she was driving her car. A potential suspect committed suicide about a month later, but the case remains open.

- John Candy and Chris Farley both died while working on films: Candy on *Wagon's East* (1994) and Farley on *Shrek* (1997) (though Farley's leading voice role in the latter was cut out of respect). *Wagon's East* was a frontier-themed comedy, and was Candy' penultimate film role, with

Canadian Bacon released posthumously. Farley's second to the last film role, *Almost Heroes*, was also a frontier-themed comedy.

- Perhaps the most believable variation of the "Paul is dead" conspiracy theory is that the Beatles made the whole thing up for a laugh and to sell more albums. Beatles' merchandise and album sales did increase quite a bit after, but the band broke up in September 1969, never to reunite.

- Another absurdity of the 1904 Summer Olympics was that the nationalities of many of the athletes were later disputed. Many of the athletes were from European countries but had lived in the United States, Canada, and Australia for so long their status was unclear.

- Although in 1999 scriptwriter Tod Carrol adamantly denied there was a curse on the production of *Atuk*, neither he nor anyone else associated with the film have made any efforts to restart production. To be honest, I don't blame them!

- When Rolling Stones founder Brian Jones died in a swimming accident at his home on July 3, 1969, he became the first member of the absurdly macabre "27 Club." The 27 Club includes rockers who died at the age of 27, usually from drug and/or alcohol overdoes, including Jimi Hendrix, Janis Joplin, Jim Morrison, Kurt Cobain, and Amy Winehouse.

- A baseball umpire's job can be quite thankless and sometimes dangerous, but did you know that if a pitch gets stuck in his face mask, all runners on base advance one base? Apparently, umps have to take the blame for their wardrobe malfunctions as well.

CHAPTER 3:

WEIRD SCIENCE

As we continue our journey through the absurd, we take a turn into the downright bizarre as we take a look at some truly strange science facts. From animals to chemistry, and from human anatomy to medicine, there's something here that'll definitely make you scratch your head and say "hmmm."

We like to think that in the current year we have most things figured out as a society, but as you'll see in this chapter there are still some scientific facts that are truly absurd and, in many ways, defy logic.

Males Aren't Needed Here

As much as birds, mammals, reptiles, and fish are very different classes of animals, they all share one common feature - they all need females *and* males to reproduce, right?

Well, that's not entirely true.

Most animals do need input from males and females to reproduce, but there's an absurd exception to this rule among reptiles.

The genus of North American lizards known as *Aspidoscelis*, which includes the New Mexico whiptail lizard and the desert grassland whiptail lizard, don't need dudes to keep their species going. Whiptail lizards reproduce through an absurdly strange biological process known as parthenogenesis, where the embryo is developed through an unfertilized egg.

Besides whiptail lizards, several other animals - such as Komodo dragons, some sharks, insects, and even some birds - can also reproduce asexually through parthenogenesis, but it's quite rare, with sexual reproduction being the norm.

Before any of you ladies reading this think this could be the answer to Earth's problems, think again. It appears that parthenogenesis is quite a primitive trait, as there are no known instances of any mammal species ever using it.

So, I guess that means you ladies are stuck with males for a while if you want to keep humanity going, at least until we devolve into lizards.

Thinking Yourself to Death

You probably know from experience that thinking too much about a problem usually only makes it worse. You keep thinking and thinking about it, and before you know it, you can't sleep or eat. Usually, that's about the worse that happens, though, at least until the problem is resolved.

But there's a really rare and bizarre condition where you actually can think yourself to death.

The medical term for "thinking yourself to death" is known as psychogenic death or psychosomatic death, or by its creepier yet cooler sounding nickname, "voodoo death."

This affliction is often called voodoo death because the earliest recorded cases were usually connected to curses in non-Western countries. The first scholar to research psychosomatic death was American physiologist Walter Cannon, who did his research among the Māori people in the early 20th century. Cannon's research uncovered that in many cases where Māori people believed they were cursed, and who were by all accounts healthy before the encounter, they would later die with undiagnosed causes of death.

Cannon argued that the death was the result of many different factors that were exacerbated by extreme, chronic anxiety over the curse. Without getting into the biological jargon, Cannon's thesis held that people facing these existential fears basically overthought everything to death, literally.

Cannon's theory was accepted throughout academia. After all, this was the same guy who came up with the "fight-or-flight" theory, so he must be right about this, they thought.

In the decades since Cannon's work was first published, a litany of scholars has challenged the reasons he stated why psychosomatic death occurs, but not the idea of it.

It should be pointed out that psychosomatic death is not limited to people from non-Western countries who are often seen as being more "superstitious." An incredible case was documented by Doctor Clifton Meador, who in a 1992 paper discussed how he treated a man who believed he was dying from cancer. When the man died, an autopsy was performed, but no signs of cancer were detected.

The most absurd thing about the man's death was that his body was perfectly healthy. Meador determined that the man *thought* himself to death.

They say that if you wish for something enough, it will come true. Of course, this saying is usually in reference to things like love, money, or success in life, but in some very rare cases, some people literally think themselves to death.

Seahorses, Cockroaches, and Rhino Horns

From afflictions of the mind, we move on to some ancient Chinese medicinal remedies that, at first glance, will make most Westerners cringe a bit. China is home to one of the world's oldest and most successful civilizations and today has nearly 1.5 billion people, so it must be doing some things right.

The modern Chinese people have readily adopted Western medicine, along with other Western concepts, but they still hold onto many of their traditional methods, some of which have been accepted by the outside world.

Acupuncture is an ancient Chinese traditional healing method that you've probably heard about and maybe even tried yourself. I know many people who've tried acupuncture and a couple who swear by its efficacy. Proponents of acupuncture admit that turning your body into a pincushion may look strange, but that it does wonders for pain and discomfort.

But what about chowing down on dried seahorses, or drinking snake venom?

Have you ever eaten bear testicles to help get "in the mood"?

Chances are you haven't, and probably don't feel the need to, no matter how interesting this all may sound. Let's take a look at some of these truly unique Chinese medical prescriptions so you won't have to eat any deer sinews or dried lizards.

Speaking of dried animals, if you ever get the chance to visit a traditional Chinese market, be sure to look for dried seahorse on a stick. That's right, it may not be cotton candy on a stick, but dried seahorse is considered a true treat among many Chinese, especially men, who believe that grinding them into powder and mixing them with their tea is a cure-all for many afflictions, including asthma, arthritis, and incontinence.

And many men swear that dried seahorse works better than Viagra!

One of the most controversial ancient Chinese medical materials is rhinoceros' horns. As with seahorses, rhino horns are grounded up into powder and added to a variety of elixirs. Although many people in the West believe rhino horns are consumed as an aphrodisiac, they are most often used as a fever remedy as it's believed the powder can "cool the blood."

There is a plethora of ancient Chinese medical prescriptions that call for the consumption of insects. Dried and powdered weaver ants are thought to alleviate asthma while eating cockroaches is believed to be a cure for strokes and high blood pressure.

As unlikely as some of these remedies may seem to many of us, before you laugh, consider that the Chinese have been consuming them for more than 3,000 years in some cases. So, all those people who've been using these remedies for so long can't be totally wrong, right?

I guess the next time I get a headache I'll make sure to drink some snake venom wine and let you guys know how it turned out.

Mr. Hiccups

Charles Osborne was a regular, Midwestern guy in 1922. He owned a farm in Iowa where he took care of his crops and livestock, which is what he was doing when his historic case of the hiccups began.

"I was hanging a 350-pound hog for butchering," Osborne said. "I picked it up and then I fell down. I felt nothing, but the doctor said later that I busted a blood vessel the size of a pin in my brain."

The result was that when Osborne was injured attempting to pick that hog up, the tiny busted blood vessel began a hiccup-filled odyssey that lasted 68 years.

Well, I'm probably being a bit overdramatic by calling it an odyssey, but can you imagine having the hiccups that long? I can't even imagine how difficult it must've been, which makes the fact that Osborne married twice, had eight children, and lived to the ripe old age of 97 all that more fascinating.

When the hiccups started, Osborne tried everything from gargling salt water to holding his breath, but nothing seemed to work. He was eventually able to limit his hiccups, though, from 40 a minute to 20. By the time Osborne died in 1991, it's estimated he had hiccupped over 430 million times over 68 years.

But as absurd as this story is, as suddenly as Osborne's hiccups started in 1922, they stopped in 1990, about one year before he died.

So, you're probably wondering how was it even possible for Osborne to have hiccups that long?

Unfortunately, there's no real answer to that question because hiccups remain somewhat of a scientific enigma. We know that the physical act of a hiccup involves a spasm of the diaphragm, but the causes are many and some are not fully understood. Also, modern drugs have only demonstrated minimal effectiveness to cure particularly tough cases of hiccups.

Experts say that if you do have a bad case of hiccups, your best bet is to try one of the many folk remedies. So, do a headstand and try to drink some water out of a straw, or better yet, have someone unexpectedly scare you.

It works on me every time.

This Small Animal Will Scare You to Death

If you're ever swimming off the shore of Queensland, Australia in the summer months (their summer, not northern hemisphere summer), you best beware the Irukandji jellyfish. Although the Irukandji jellyfish is no larger than the average fingernail, it packs a toxin that has been described as one of the most powerful on earth.

And it can quite literally scare you to death!

Those unfortunate enough to have been stung by the Irukandji jellyfish may not even feel the sting, but usually, within 5 to 30 minutes, victims will lapse into what's known as "Irukandji syndrome."

The initial stages of Irukandji syndrome often start with a headache and a stomach ache before progressing into increased heart rate, extreme anxiety, and a profound feeling of terror. If the victim has only suffered one or two stings, then symptoms usually dissipate in a few hours, but if the unlucky person has suffered multiple stings, then things can get worse, really quickly.

The Irukandji jellyfish is part of the larger box jellyfish family, which consists of several different species of poisonous jellyfishes. The problem is that a box jellyfish antivenom has only been recently developed, has not been proven to be effective for all box jellyfish species, and is not widely available.

In other words, if you get the Irukandji syndrome, you'll have to ride it out with other medicines.

Opioid-derived pain killers are commonly given to victims of Irukandji syndrome, as is nitroglycerin. Although death from Irukandji syndrome is rare, it can happen from multiple stings or in those who have weakened hearts because the venom flows through the circulatory system, directly affecting the heart.

The exact numbers of those killed by the sting of the Irukandji jellyfish are unknown because their sting has been attributed to other causes, and other jellyfish, but it is estimated to be about 70. I guess those aren't bad odds when you consider how many people hit the beach every year in jellyfish-infested waters.

Still, I'll be extra careful the next time I go for a swim.

Animal Magnetism Was Once Thought to Be a Real Thing

You've probably heard the term "animal magnetism" before, with reference to someone who has a powerful yet primitive charisma. People with animal magnetism are often described as physically attractive in a raw, earthy kind of way, charming in an everyman sense, and also possessing a certain dark mystique.

Animal magnetism is also often used to describe a kind of raw physical and/or sexual attraction two people have for each other sometimes. It's the kind of attraction that can't really be described in words but can be expressed in very physical ways.

But we all know the idea of animal magnetism is just some absurd thing someone made up, right?

Wrong: as absurd as the idea of animal magnetism may seem, or not seem, it does have some basis on a scientific level. It was the idea of a legitimate late 18th-century German scientist named Franz Anton Mesmer, who came up with some other ideas that were truly outside the box.

If you're wondering where you've heard Mesmer's name before, it's probably because the term "mesmerism" is named after him. Yes, Mesmer is considered by many to be the father of modern hypnotism, but that only came about due to his work on the theory of animal magnetism.

So, how did Mesmer come up with the idea of animal magnetism and how is it related to hypnotism?

Before we get to Mesmer's work, it's important to know a little bit about the man's background and the time in which he lived. Mesmer was born in 1734 in the Holy Roman Empire (basically the predecessor of modern-day Germany) and spent much of his life in that country as well as Austria and France.

The 1700s was the era known as the 'Enlightenment', when new political, social, and scientific ideas were being formulated and old ones were being questioned. So, after Mesmer enrolled at the University of Vienna in 1759, he decided to take his studies of medical science in a new direction. Mesmer focused on how the ocean tides affect the flow of blood and other fluids in the human body, which he also referred to as "tides," and eventually how human tides could affect other human tides.

Mesmer believed that if he focused his energy on the bodies of his patients, especially certain parts, he could heal their afflictions, especially mental/psychological problems.

For Mesmer, the key was successfully breaking the "barrier" or invisible magnetic force that he believed all animals had and making the biological as well as the psychological elements of the body "flow" as they were intended.

This all may seem very absurd, but the truth is Mesmer became very popular with the rich and powerful in Paris during the late 1700s. They were lined up, willing to pay big francs to sit in a chair and have Mesmer stare at them and run his hands over them, sometimes for hours.

Today, skeptics think of Mesmer as a charlatan, but his modern supporters point out that his methods and philosophy were very similar to Eastern medical styles that focus on chakras, Chi, and other concepts that describe the unseen, metaphysical force that flows through humans.

Mesmer's philosophy and methods attained wider appeal after he died in the 1800s. Practitioners became known as "magnetizers," sometimes charging large fees for therapies that consisted of laying their hands on the afflicted.

The methods Mesmer used later became the basis for hypnotism first practiced by Scottish surgeon James Braid in the mid-1800s. Braid disagreed with Mesmer on the idea of the invisible force known as animal magnetism, but he did follow a similar one-on-one therapy method that eventually evolved into modern hypnotism.

The idea of animal magnetism continued to fall out of favor after Braid, but many still follow Mesmer's ideas and practices and see nothing absurd about them. I guess one person's scientific absurdity is another's profound worldview.

The Hyena is One Weird Animal

The natural world is full of many animals that are truly head-scratchers. We've already seen how some lizards don't need males to procreate and how a tiny jellyfish can scare a person to death, so now let's take a look at the strangest species of mammal on Earth - the hyena.

Hyenas are actually a group of four species - brown hyena, aardwolf, striped hyena, and spotted hyena - that are native to Asia and Africa. Most people think hyenas are related to dogs and other canines based on their looks as well as some of their biological features, but they arc only partially correct. Hyenas do have an ancient lineage with canines, sharing features such as strong canine jaws. Actually, hyenas' jaws are even stronger than the average canine's and are capable of breaking bones. And also, like canines, hyenas don't have retractable claws, so they can't climb trees, but in a weird twist of biology, hyenas are actually in the biological suborder filiform, which makes canines their closer relatives.

As much as hyenas may look like ugly dogs, they do act like felines in some ways. Hyena's groom themselves like cats and even use communal "cat boxes" for their poop!

Another strange thing about hyenas, at least when compared to other mammals, is that they tend to be very matriarchal species.

Female hyenas run the packs and are larger than the males. The females also have more testosterone.

Males are pretty much just sperm donors in hyena society.

But as strange or absurd all of this is about hyenas in general, the spotted hyena is the strangest of all.

The spotted hyena is the one most commonly featured on nature shows due to its even weirder appearance (it resembles a cross between a bear and a dog), aggressive nature, and the sounds it makes. The very vocal spotted hyena has a wide range of sounds it makes, including whoops, groans, and of course, laughs.

The spotted hyena usually makes its famous giggling sound when it has been chased, often by another hyena, over a kill. The giggle can quickly turn to a growl, though, if the hyena decides to stand its ground.

Perhaps the strangest thing about the spotted hyena is the existence of some pretty confusing biology down below on the females.

Possibly owing to the higher levels of testosterone, female spotted hyenas have an enlarged clitoris that is six to seven inches long, resembling a pseudo-penis. The labia of spotted hyenas also appear to be fused together, looking like a scrotum.

So, how does this affect breeding? Well, let's just say that it's a delicate process for the males. They have to carefully make sure everything lines up - and in - for them to do the deed. And if all that's not wild enough, females frequently attack their mate when they're finished!

That's one weird mammal.

Fart Proof Underwear

Consider for a moment all the great inventions and scientific theories that have made life better. You have the wheel, electricity, combustion engines, bacterial theory, flight, writing, the concept of zero, anesthesia, vaccines, space exploration, and marine biology just to name a few of the great scientific achievements of the last 5,000 years.

It's hard to say where we'd be without many of those inventions, and it's also difficult to think where we'd be without fart-proof underwear.

Well, not really on the last thing, but believe it or not, a guy named Chester "Buck" Weimer of Pueblo, Colorado received a patent for odor-proof undies in 1998.

Weimer was a man with a plan to combat his wife Arlene's flatulence problem. All jokes aside, Mrs. Weimer suffered from Crohn's disease, which gives the afflicted frequent gas. So, according to Weimer, the night after a Thanksgiving dinner, as he listened and smelled the flatulence coming from his wife sleeping next to him, he decided that he'd do something to help everyone in her situation.

There's also no doubt he was compelled to help himself.

After doing some brainstorming, and then experimenting, Weimer made a charcoal filter lining for underwear that reduces the smell of the farts, but not necessarily the sounds. Well, the first one is always the worst if you're on the receiving end and the second can be a bit of a laugh, so I guess it was a success.

Weimer's fart-proof underwear earned him the respect of inventors around the world - enough so that he was awarded the somewhat sarcastic Ig Noble Prize for Biology in 2001. The fart-proof underwear has been a modest financial success as well, although there certainly is a very big market for the product.

Buck Weimer is proof that not every scientist works in a high-tech lab and not every inventor devises lifesaving machines. Some people work out of their homes to make the world a bit less smelly, which if you ask me, isn't so absurd.

Strange but True Science Facts

- Charles Osborne doesn't have a monopoly on absurd life circumstances involving hiccups. In 2007, Florida teenager Jennifer Mee gained national attention when she revealed her case of unending hiccups to the media. Although Mee's hiccups went away, her troubles didn't when she was convicted for a 2010 murder and sentenced to life in prison.

- As mentioned earlier, Anton Mesmer's ideas of "body energy" were not necessarily new. Ancient Chinese medicine asserts, very much like Mesmer did, that the human body has a fundamental substance called *Qi* that makes everything move. Traditional Chinese medicine also holds that all human organs are influenced by five substances: wood, fire, metal, earth, and water.

- You may be surprised to learn that over 99% of the volume of flatus (a fart) is actually odorless gas. Scientists have learned that what causes the stink is a combination of sulfur compounds. Since it's less than 1% that can do some pretty serious olfactory damage, I'd hate to smell what a full 1% could do.

- Hyenas give birth to two to three young at a time, which are called cubs. Hyena cubs actually look kind of cute, considering how tough they appear when they become adults.

- Psychosomatic or voodoo death should not be confused with a panic attack. Panic attacks are sudden and intense, while voodoo death usually takes place over a prolonged period.

Also, as bad as a panic attack may seem if you have one, and as much as it may seem like you're dying, they are not fatal.

- The first known case of parthenogenesis in a shark was observed in 2001 in a bonnethead shark in the Henry Doorly Zoo in Omaha, Nebraska.

- Mesmer was a true product of the Enlightenment, making connections with such notable people as composer Wolfgang Amadeus Mozart.

- The ancient Egyptians had an interesting relationship with hyenas. Unlike other felines and canines, hyenas weren't sacred animals, so they didn't have the same protection. It's believed some were tamed (not domesticated) and possibly used as guard animals, while others may have been eaten. Needless to say, there are no ancient Egyptian texts that describe hyena as a choice dish.

- Scientists are perplexed as to why some people are repelled by others' flatulence but have no problems with - or even seem to enjoy - their own. It may have to do with an ancient survival technique that's been carried on into modern times, but chances are we'll probably never know why your little brother likes to pull the covers over his head after he passes gas!

- The Irukandji jellyfish is native to Australia, but there are reports it's made its way as far north as Japan, Britain, and the US.

CHAPTER 4:

OUTRAGEOUS
LITERATURE AND ART

At first, the words "outrageous" or "absurd" may not come to your mind when you think of literature and art. The people who enjoy those things tend to be a bit more on the refined side and to many people, the subject matter can often be boring. But once you peel that first layer away, you quickly begin to see just how absurd the world of art and literature can really be.

Let's face it, artists and writers are some of the most eccentric people on the face of the Earth. In fact, I think the word "eccentric" was probably invented to describe them!

And not only that, these eccentric artists and writers have been inspired by some pretty absurd things and have produced some works that have proven to be as jaw-dropping and head-scratching as they are engaging.

So, let's delve into eight of the most absurd stories from the world of literature and art.

Now That's a Lot of Words

If you're reading this, there's a good chance, you're a book worm, and since this is a non-fiction book, there's also a good chance that's your cup of reading tea. But novels are where the big money is, as they are the type of books that sell the most and overwhelmingly get turned into television and film scripts.

And chances are you've read more than a few novels in your time and at least one of them was absurdly long.

Perhaps you read Leo Tolstoy's *War and Peace* in your college literature class. If so, you should've received extra credit if you made it through all 600,000 words.

Or maybe you tackled Stephen King's 514,827-word *The Stand* during one of your summer breaks.

Or possibly you wanted to know why your cousin was getting into Scientology, so you dedicated several weeks of your life to reading L. Ron Hubbard's ten-volume, 1,200,000-word, *Mission Earth*.

But as absurdly long as those novels are, they're nothing compared to those at the top of the list.

For a long time, the 17th-century French novel, *Artamène ou le Grand Cyrus* (*Cyrus the Great*), was believed to be the longest novel in the world. Written by Georges de Scudéry, or possibly his sister Madeleine, *Artamène* checks in at a spellbinding 1,954,300 words in ten volumes.

Other writers have claimed their books to be longer than *Artamène*, but the problem is the question of when a work is truly one novel in several volumes, and when those different volumes consist of different works. This is the question that plagued Englishman Henry Williamson's 15-volume set, *A Chronicle of Ancient Sunlight*. *Chronicle* has 2,436,924 words total, so it beats *Artamène,* but many people consider it a series and not multiple volumes of the same novel.

Whether you considered *Artamène* or *Chronicle* to be the longest novel in history, both were finally beaten in 2020 when Indian writer Bahuleyan Jeyamohan finally released his 26-volume magnum opus, *Venmurasu*. At more than 3.5 million words, *Venmurasu* blows away all comers in verbosity. The novel is a retelling of the ancient Hindu epic the *Mahabharata,* but don't get your hopes up to read it unless you know Tamil.

As absurdly long as these novels are, I can almost guarantee a longer book will be published someday. Maybe someone is writing that novel right now!

How Destruction Inspired Art

The great artistic masterpieces of history have found many sources of inspiration. The sculptors and painters of the Renaissance were influenced by the beauty of the human body and the styles of the much earlier Greek and Roman artists.

Artists in the ancient and medieval worlds were driven by a deep desire to connect with their god or gods.

But beauty or a yearning to connect with a higher power aren't the only things that inspire masterpieces. As absurd as it may seem, destruction and even death have been the inspiration for some of the greatest works of art in the modern world.

You've probably seen an image of Norwegian expressionist Edvard Munch's 1893 painting, *The Scream*. It's the painting where an androgynous, almost alien-looking person has their hands on the side of their face as they let out a scream on what appears to be a pier. There's a couple of people walking in the background, but what's most noticeable is the bright orange-red sky.

In typical Scandinavian fashion, Munch never commented very much on the painting, only saying that the inspiration came from within and was an expression of how he was feeling at the time. Munch was, after all, an Expressionist painter, and *The Scream* is considered a classic Expressionist work.

But many art historians believe that although Munch's feelings may have been genuine, another inspiration for *The Scream* was the 1883 volcanic eruption on the island of Krakatoa in Indonesia. Krakatoa was the deadliest, most destructive volcano in modern history, killing more than 36,000 people and all but wiping out the island. Art historians point out that the red skies in *The Scream* are eerily similar to the skies seen over much of the southern hemisphere after the eruption of Krakatoa.

Still, not all art historians are convinced. Some think it's absurd that an Expressionist of Munch's stature would lower himself to using something so physical and mundane as a volcano for a subject of one of his masterpieces.

I guess the answer comes down to what you believe is more absurd but remember that when it comes to being absurd, writers and artists can't be beat!

Ray Bradbury Was Huge in the Soviet Union

Long before George Lucas became a household name with the *Star Wars* epics and just prior to Philip K. Dick scaring his readers with numerous dystopian visions of the future, Ray Bradbury was *the* American science fiction writer. In many ways, Bradbury made sci-fi mainstream and cool at the same time and also started a trend of turning top-selling short stories and books into television shows and movies.

Bradbury's writing style and abilities were as far-ranging as his audience, as he produced epics such as *The Martian Chronicles* as well as profound, timeless pieces, like *Fahrenheit 451*.

From the time he got his first story published in 1938 until his death in 2012, Bradbury was known for amazing his fans with fantasy worlds that seemed so different, but often so similar to our own. Bradbury also became known for stirring controversy by pushing the envelope on political correctness and often questioning the order of things.

So, when you consider Ray Bradbury's background, it may seem pretty absurd that he was the most popular writer in the Soviet Union during its last three decades.

Not Karl Marx.

Not Friedrich Engels.

But Ray Bradbury, the "capitalist American pig" who penned *Fahrenheit 451*, which in case you don't know, is about a totalitarian government that routinely burned books. Many believed it was a direct attack on the Soviet Union and its censorship policies.

So, with that in mind, how did Bradbury become so popular in the Soviet Union?

Part of the answer to that can be found in the nature of the Soviet system and the nature of humans everywhere, no matter their backgrounds. The Soviet Union actively pursued a policy of censorship on the one hand and promoted its own vision of the world in art and literature on the other. Soviet science fiction tended to be happy, rosy, full of political platitudes, and quite frankly, boring.

So, Soviet sci-fi just didn't sell well with the key demographic of younger people, who once they found out about Bradbury, did whatever they could to read his works. And the more the Soviet authorities censored Bradbury, and therefore, came to resemble the firemen in *Fahrenheit 451*, the more popular he became.

Unofficial Ray Bradbury clubs could be found from Leningrad (St. Petersburg) to Moscow and Kiev Club members would discuss their favorite Bradbury stories and the implications they had on the future. In addition to Bradbury's better-known sci-fi stories, the non-sci-fi 1957 novel *Dandelion Wine*, which depicts coming of age in the 1928 Midwest, was also extremely popular.

But Bradbury's absurd popularity on the other side of the Iron Curtain wasn't just relegated to the kids.

Bradbury was himself an admirer of the Russian people, so when acclaimed Soviet film director Sergei Bondarchuk was in Hollywood in 1968 to accept an Academy Award for his film version of the novel *War and Peace*, Bradbury thought he'd go and get a peek at the director.

Bradbury was already successful and famous in his own right, but he was one of many people among a crowd of Hollywood A-list actors, directors, and producers at the ceremony that night. But Bondarchuk looked through the crowd and noticed Bradbury.

According to Bradbury, he said, "Ray Bradbury, is that you?" Then called him over to his table.

It turns out Bondarchuk was a big fan of Bradbury and claimed he influenced some of his work. It seems pretty absurd that an American who wrote a dystopian novel about censorship would become one of the most popular writers in the Soviet Union, but as Bradbury often stressed in his work, sometimes things aren't always as they seem.

Art at the Olympics

Earlier we looked at how absurd the marathon was at the 1904 Summer Olympics, with performance-enhancing drugs, brazen cheating, and some colorful competitors all making it a weird competition that the organizers probably wanted to forget. But as absurd as the 1904 marathon was, it wasn't the only absurd thing that took place during the early modern Olympics.

Did you know that they had art competitions in the Summer Olympics from 1912 through 1948?

For most of us today, it just sounds absurd on the face of it, mixing art and sports. When I was growing up, the jocks were one group and the art kids were another, and it seems like that's still the same way today.

But it wasn't always this way.

The ancient Greeks freely mixed art and athletics and when Pierre de Coubertin first came up with the idea of the modern Olympics in the late 1800s, he wanted to follow the Greek example as much as possible. So, beginning in 1912, the Olympics began welcoming artists to compete for prizes.

There were five major categories — architecture, literature, music, painting, and sculpture - with all but architecture having subcategories and literature having several, including dramatic, epic, and lyrics.

I know what you're wondering, "How could they actually have an art competition at an international sporting event?"

Well, the art competition was usually held at a museum or pavilion in the host city, and there were some rules the competitors had to follow. Athleticism had to be the subject of each piece, which included music compositions and literature.

I think it helps to remember that this was the early and mid-20th century, long before the era of professional sports dominance of today. In other words, the Olympic artists weren't making songs or writing stories about the Minnesota Vikings or Manchester United. No, these were works of art that glorified the *concepts* of competition, athleticism, and sportsmanship.

When you put that into perspective, it's not so absurd.

The artists were judged by professional juries and awarded medals just like the athletes, but sometimes there weren't enough competitors in every category.

The art competitions were a bit of novelty for the first few Olympics but perhaps unsurprisingly became quite popular at the 1924 games in Paris. After all, Paris is the city of art, right? Art competitions at the Olympics peaked during the 1928 games in Amsterdam when more than 1,000 pieces were entered into the competition.

But the idea was doomed to fail in many ways.

The Great Depression was the first blow to art at the Olympics, then came World War II. After the War, society had changed with the rise of popular professional sports leagues around the world. People began to see sports in a different light and by the 1950s, the idea of sports and art mixing seemed like an absurd concept to many, if not most people.

The International Olympic Committee (IOC) also began seeing art at the Olympics as an absurdity. They argued that since many of the artists who competed were professional artists, and many actually sold their pieces once the games were over, they should be eliminated from a competition that was in theory supposed to promote amateurism.

And that's probably the biggest absurdity of this entire story. The IOC eliminated art competitions due to the money changing hands but today the Olympics are among the largest money-making enterprises in the world, and professionals compete in several competitions.

Chris Burden Was Truly a Weird Guy

The word "eccentric" is interesting. By its most basic definition, it can mean "strange" or even "troubled"; but it's almost always used to refer to writers, artists, and occasionally very rich people.

The homeless drug addict who talks to himself and panhandles outside your apartment building is never referred to as eccentric, is he?

Nor is your alcoholic aunt who always seems to ruin Thanksgiving dinner.

No, "eccentric" is reserved for artists and writers who would otherwise be called mentally unwell for their behaviors.

And some of them had some pretty strange behavior.

You probably know about Vincent van Gogh's eccentric, more like erratic behavior that culminated with him severing his left ear on the cold lonely night of December 23, 1888. Then there was Andy Warhol, who was one of the weirdest artists of his era. He collected a cadre of like-minded artists at a collective known as the Factory, which ended up in him getting shot, but not killed, by a radical feminist who wanted to destroy the patriarchy.

That's actually quite ironic because Warhol was about the least patriarchal of all men at the time.

Anyways, the point is that many of the best-known artists, of any time, are eccentric/strange people, and this is true of lesser-known artists as well, such as Chris Burden.

Chris Burden was born in 1946 to a well-educated family who traveled the world for their work in academia. Young Chris was exposed to many different ideas and people, but he was particularly drawn to art. He entered the University of California, Irvine in the early 1970s as an art student, and almost immediately he began making a name for himself.

Burden's preferred style was performance art, and his medium was film, which by the early '70s both were becoming popular in the post-counterculture art communities in urban areas across the US. Some of Burden's performance pieces included him not eating for several days or attempting to survive for several days in remote locations.

Strange, but not too strange, right?

Well, his weirdest and most controversial pieces involved guns. As politically liberal and pro-gun-control as many modern artists tend to be, Burden bucked that trend somewhat by featuring guns in some of his most important works.

Burden is probably best known for his 1971 film *Shoot*, where he filmed himself being shot in the shoulder with a .22 caliber rifle. After being patched up at a local hospital, Burden faced the art critics, only saying that the piece was a reflection of violence in television, but not necessarily an indictment of it.

Shoot made Burden famous, so he did as any truly eccentric artist would do by following it up with something even crazier.

In 1973, Burden filmed *747*, which was a film of him standing on a beach and firing a gun at a plane taking off from Los Angeles International Airport.

747 also proved to be a hit with the art crowd, but it also became popular with the FBI, who had some serious questions for the very eccentric artist.

Burden later claimed that he told the FBI that *747* was "about the goodness of man — the idea that you can't regulate everybody. At the airport, everybody's being searched for guns, and here I am on the beach and it looks like I'm plucking planes out of the sky. You can't regulate the world."

Okay, I guess that sort of explanation would work in 1973, but we all know what wouldn't cut it today.

After *747*, Burden's work was noticeably less dangerous to others, although he continued to push his own body to the limits. He had himself crucified on the hood of a Volkswagen

Beetle in 1974's *Trans-Fixed*, which was the best known of his self-inflicted harm pieces of the mid-1970s.

By the late 1970s, Burden's violent self-harm pieces had lost popularity in the art scene, not to mention he was getting older, so he turned to the safer style of sculpture.

To those who are not familiar with Chris Burden or his unique style, he's thought of as absurd, weird, and a little, or a lot, unhinged. But for many artists and art lovers, Chris Burden will always be remembered as an eccentric artist who pushed the limits of his body and what was acceptable in the art world.

So, it comes down to your choice whether Burden was mentally unwell or eccentric.

Film, Literature, and Esperanto

The search for a worldwide *lingua franca* has been an ongoing process for more than 2,000 years, with several strange and some would say absurd twists and turns along the way. But before we examine one of the more interesting of these absurd linguistic turns, let's consider what a *lingua franca* is.

The literal translation of the Latin term, *lingua franca* is "French language." The term generally refers to a language that is the common medium by which people of different languages communicate. Today English is the de facto *lingua franca* of the world. In the 1700s, however, French was the most commonly known language, so it became the *lingua franca*, thus the term, but there were others before it.

Akkadian was the *lingua franca* of the Late Bronze Age Near East (c. 1500-1200 BCE), and Greek was the *lingua franca* of the

Mediterranean and Near East during the Hellenistic Period (330-31 BCE). French, Akkadian, and Greek all shared some common attributes: they were existing languages, and they became dominant through the influence of a powerful state/kingdom.

By the late 1800s, as the world was pretty much between *lingua francas*, a Polish ophthalmologist named Ludwik Zamenhof decided he would make a new *lingua franca* from scratch.

Besides being an eye doctor, Zamenhof was a philologist who wrote a Yiddish grammar book in 1879, so he certainly had the background to create a new language. Borrowing heavily from Spanish, Italian, and other Romance languages, but also employing English, German, and Yiddish words and syntax, Zamenhof introduced his new language, which he called *Esperanto*, to the world in 1887.

There was an initial interest in Esperanto, but it was primarily limited to authors and later other artists. Several authors have written entirely or almost entirely in Esperanto, including Briton William Auld, who was nominated for a Noble Prize in Literature.

Perhaps the most interesting aspect of what some think is an absurd turn in linguistic history is the production of four films in Esperanto. *Angoroj* (*Agonies*) was the first Esperanto language film to hit the big screen in 1964. It was followed up a year later by the horror film *Incubus*, starring William Shatner. Yes, *the* William Shatner of Captain Kirk-*Star Trek* fame starred in a cheesy, low-budget film about female demons who seduce men and take them into Hell. It's doubtful you've seen *Incubus* on any late-night movie channels, though, as it was lost until 1996, has never been dubbed, and only recently had English subtitles added.

But Captain Kirk wasn't big enough to make Esperanto catch on. Only two other Esperanto language feature films were ever made. The Brazilian film company Imagu-filmoj produced *Gerda Malaperis!* (*Gerda Disappeared!*) in 2006 and *La patro* (*The Father*) in 2007, but it's been crickets since.

It now appears that Esperanto will never become the *lingua franca* Zamenhof had hoped, and maybe it was absurd to even think so. There are still some things you can do with the language, though. Maybe you'll write the next great Esperanto novel or produce an Esperanto film.

And as Esperantists would say, bonŝancon!

She Paid How Much for Nothing?

So far in this book we've seen that absurdity, just like beauty and what constitutes art, is often in the eyes of the beholder. But no matter how absurd, or ugly, the piece in question may be, there's always something to look at.

Until actor James Franco created his "masterpiece" *Fresh Air*.

In 2011, Franco gave his financial support, and his "artistic talents," to a new museum in New York City called the Museum of Non-Visible Art. Yes, that's the actual name of the place, and yes, it is a building full of nothing - at least, not any art in the physical sense. As absurd as this sounds, I guess I'll just let the people from the museum itself describe it:

"Composed entirely of ideas, the work that the Museum of Non-Visible Art showcases remains unseen. Although the artworks themselves are not visible, the descriptions are readable, and open our eyes to a parallel world built of images and words."

74

Okay, so it has little cards that "describe" each piece, but the funny thing is, you can just go to the website to read them!

And as absurd as this story is, it got even more absurd not long after the place opened.

A woman named Aimee Davison actually paid $10,000 for an original Franco "sculpture" called *Fresh Air*. She got a card that described the piece and plenty of media attention. It turns out that Davison probably really likes attention as she's worked as a news media producer and "sold her soul" in 2011 to some guy on Craigslist.

Eccentric, bizarre, or plain silly…take your pick!

If you're bummed out that *Fresh Air* is no longer on the market and you still want an original James Franco, don't worry, the museum also has a Franco "cloth" called *Slave Costume*, a "film" titled *Red Leaves*, and another "sculpture" named *Boat of Captain*.

I'm not sure if Franco is trolling everyone with this, or if his many stoner flicks have seeped into reality, but this is one of the most absurd cases of "art" in history.

Bound in Skin

The art of writing was first invented in ancient Mesopotamia and Egypt (more or less simultaneously and independently) more than 5,000 years ago. In those early years, the people of those civilizations didn't have a whole lot to work with in terms of writing materials. The Egyptians wrote their texts on a reed known as papyrus or on the walls of their tombs and temples, while the Mesopotamians were a bit more limited. They primarily wrote on cooked clay blocks.

The media on which people wrote changed little over the next several thousand years. Papyrus was the most popular medium in Europe and the Middle East, but as the papyrus began running out scholars were forced to look elsewhere.

Europeans began using animal skins, which proved to be quite adaptable. And then somewhere along the line, someone got the idea of using *human* skin as a writing medium.

The technical term for binding a book in human skin is "anthropodermic bibliopegy," and as "medieval" as it may sound, it's actually kind of modern.

The earliest known reference to a book bound in human skin is a 1710 book titled *Molleri manuale præparationis ad mortem*, although this was only a reference, and the actual book has not been located.

There were numerous references to books being bound in the skin of the victims of the Reign of Terror during the French Revolution (1789-1799). It appears that after they lost their heads in the guillotine, they were then flayed in the name of liberty!

The vast majority of books that people claim to have been bound in human skin, and those that have been proven to be thanks to modern testing techniques, are from the 1800s. This is quite bizarre and absurd when you consider that paper as we know it today began being used for books in the late Middle Ages and that in the 1800s, there was no lack of paper. The most famous of these are 1800s reprints, in human skin, of the 1500s woodcuts of English artist Hans Holbein's *Dance of Death*.

As absurd and creepy as the idea of books bound in human skin is, they fetch big bucks on the auction block. So, who knows, the next time you help clean out the attic of your deceased, creepy relative, there may be a macabre book in there worth a fortune.

Strange but True Literature and Art Facts

- Another notable masterpiece that was inspired by destruction was Pablo Picasso's *Guernica*. The painting depicts, in the very Picassoesque Cubist style, the 1937 bombing of the Spanish town of Guernica by the German air force during the Spanish Civil War.

- Hungarian Alfréd Hajós is the only Olympian to have medaled in both athletics and art. He won gold at the 1896 Summer Olympics in Athens for the 100-meter and 1,200-meter freestyle swimming events and a silver medal in architecture at the 1924 games in Paris.

- The cryptocurrency Monero gets its name from the Esperanto word for money, "mono."

- When it comes to the absurd in literature, and life for that matter, many think counterculture writer Hunter S. Thompson neatly summed it up when he said, "When the going gets weird the weird go pro."

- Iraqi dictator Saddam Hussein claimed to have had the Quran written in his blood. He supposedly had 50 to 57 pints drained from his body for the bizarre publication, although the copy has never been located and some doubt its existence.

- Today, paper is made from pulp. The earliest known paper made from the pulp was produced in China in the 2nd century CE, but the idea didn't make it to Europe until the 1200s.

- Jack London and Mark Twain were also popular American authors in the Soviet Union. The Soviet government liked to interpret the writings of foreign writers as pro-socialist, which in the case of London was not too difficult, but it was a bit of a stretch for Mark Twain.

- The Esperanto title of *Incubus* is *Inkubo*. Although many Esperantists praised the film for being done completely in Esperanto, others criticized the actors' pronunciation of the contrived language.

- Germany brought home the most medals in Olympic art competitions with 23 total and also led all other nations with seven gold medals in art.

- Many people believe the *Necronomicon* is another example of a book bound in human skin, but it was a fictional grimoire, totally the invention of American sci-fi/horror writer, H.P. Lovecraft.

CHAPTER 5:

WACKY GEOGRAPHY

We continue our trip through the world's absurd to all points of the globe, literally. In this chapter, we'll take a look at some strange places and other geographical oddities, from scary bridges to creepy islands. We'll see just how weird some often-overlooked places on our planet can be.

The Earth may not be very large compared to some other planets in our solar system, but it's more than big enough to house plenty of geographic mysteries.

Enter This Island at Your Own Risk

There are several forbidden areas in the world, where people are prohibited by governments from entering. Usually, these exclusion zones are established for our own good: they are full of pollution, radiation, or dangerous wild animals.

But there's one island in the Bay of Bengal that's off-limits because of its unwelcoming inhabitants.

North Sentinel Island is just one of many islands in the Andaman Islands archipelago, which although Indian territory is actually closer to the country of Myanmar, about 81 miles off its shore. There aren't any resources on North Sentinel Island anyone in the modern world really needs, so it and its people have been left alone, isolated.

And that's just the way the Sentinelese people like it.

Since 1956, laws have protected the Sentinelese people by prohibiting any outsiders from coming within five miles of its shores. The Indian government, the United Nations, and other organizations say that this is because the Sentinelese people have no immunity to modern diseases since they've had no contact with outsiders for nearly their entire existence.

But the truth is the laws are also there to protect anyone who for whatever reason feels the need to visit the Sentinelese.

The Sentinelese have routinely shown belligerence toward any outsiders even getting remotely close to their island. When officials flew over there in helicopters after the 2004 earthquake and tsunami, the Sentinelese threw spears and shot arrows at the hovering copter.

By that point, most people knew that North Sentinel Island was a no-go zone, but it didn't stop a couple of Indian fishermen from getting too close to the island in 2006.

It was the last fishing trip the two men took!

But the most absurd incident on North Sentinel Island involved the visit of 26-year-old American missionary, John Chau, in 2018. Chau knew the risks involved. He knew that he could go to jail in India just for visiting the island, but more importantly, he knew about the defensive nature of the Sentinelese people. But Chau was intent on proselytizing to them, as they knew nothing about Christianity, or really anything else about the modern world. So, he learned as much of the language as he could and bribed some fishermen to bring him to the island.

Chau almost immediately made contact with the Sentinelese, and it wasn't good. They actually shot his Bible with an arrow, but he still attempted to convert the people.

It was the last mission Chau ever made.

The fisherman who brought Chau to the island said they later saw some Sentinelese dragging his body on the beach and burying it.

To all of us who live in the modern world, North Sentinel Island may seem like a strange place, but when I think of all the problems we have in our world, I don't think it's so absurd after all that the Sentinelese people just want to be left alone.

The Shortest Runway in the World

The fear of flying, or pteromerhanophobia, is quite common and chances are that more than a few of you reading this suffer from the affliction. For some people, the fear begins in the airport and doesn't end until they're safely back on land. I guess that's why bars are common in most airports and most doctors are more than willing to prescribe Xanax to anxiety-prone patients with upcoming flights.

But for most people, anxiety is a matter of degrees and most of the fear happens on take-off and landing, which is probably because that's when most disasters happen.

So, if you don't like flying, and really had the take-offs and landings, there are a few to avoid.

The super short and super scary airport in Gibraltar, which is right under the famous Rock of Gibraltar, is both scenic and scary if you have flying anxiety. But you have to travel to the Caribbean to find the scariest runways.

The Princess Juliana International Airport is the main airport on the Dutch Caribbean Island of Saint Martin, so if you're headed there for a little sun and fun, be sure to look out the window before you land (if landings don't frighten you). You'll probably be amazed and possibly terrified, at the people below on Maho Beach getting blown away, literally, by the jets taking off and landing.

Since Princess Juliana's runway is so short at 7,546 feet, jets fly only 30 to 60 feet above the beach!

But as bad as the Princess Juliana runway may be, many people think the Juancho E. Yrausquin Airport is the worst.

Located a few hundred miles from St. Martin on the Dutch Caribbean Island of Saba (I think there's a theme with the Dutch Caribbean islands being scary), the airport, which serves a population of fewer than 2,000 people, is believed to be the smallest in the world.

And a small airport is sure to have a small runway, right?

The runway of the airport is the shortest commercial runway in the world at only 1,312 feet. And to make matters worse, one end of the runway ends on the foot of the mountain while the other abruptly drops off into the ocean!

Personally, I'm not afraid of flying, but if I ever get offered a vacation to Saba, I'll go by boat.

Gravity Hills

What goes up must come down, right? That's the simplest way that a simple guy like me can explain the concept of gravity, which Isaac Newton described much more eloquently more than 300 years ago. It's called the *law* of gravity because it's always true, without doubt, 100% of the time.

But there are quite a few places in the world that seem to defy the laws of gravity.

These locations - some isolated and some in quite densely-populated areas - are known as "gravity hills" or "magnetic hills" because they seemingly defy the laws of gravity. Water seems to flow uphill at these locations, and in the ones where there are roads, you can even put your car in neutral and go uphill!

You can find gravity hills on every continent (minus Antarctica that we know of so far) and in the larger countries, you'll find several. There's a good chance there's one near you and maybe you didn't even know about it.

There's the aptly named Spook Hill on US Route 27 near Orlando, Florida that attracts more than a few interested tourists every day to see if they really can put their cars in neutral and go uphill. And if you go to Lewisberry, Pennsylvania, you'll find a "T" intersection just outside the town where the laws of gravity seem to be suspended.

But my favorite gravity hill is actually a gravity hill-type theme park called the Cosmos Mystery Area near Rapid City in the Black Hills. Visitors watch in amazement as balls and water go uphill, making the place truly seem like a cosmos onto itself.

So, what gives? Are there magnetic forces under the Earth in certain places that can pull objects up against gravity? Or is there something more ominous at work?

People used to think it was one of those two things or both, but now we know gravity hills are an absurdly quirky combination of geography and optical science.

There's no doubt that gravity hills are very special geographic locations, but they're that way primarily because the horizon is obstructed, usually by trees. The balance mechanism in our inner ears also plays a role in these absurd places, as objects that we expect to be vertical really aren't.

I guess you could say the only thing really absurd about gravity hills is the way our brains look at them.

The First and Shortest Place Name

If you do enough travel, you begin to notice that the names of places are as unique as the topography and people who inhabit them. You have places named for waterfalls, rivers, and mountains, while in other places they are named after leaders.

Many cities in the US are named after earlier cities in the ancient world, such as Rome, Athens, Sparta, Memphis, and Corinth, just to name a few. You also have many places in North America, as well as Australia and New Zealand, that have retained their pre-European place names, giving the locations an often-ancient heritage.

And as you look at the various place names, you may find yourself searching for the shortest place names in the world. You'll learn there are only 30-plus one-letter named locations in the world. Some of these places include the "D" River in Oregon, which claims to be the shortest river in the world.

There are also a number of places named "U" in the world, primarily in Asian countries, a few "Y"s, and a spattering of "O"s, but by far the most popular one-letter place name also happens to be the first letter, well sort of, Å.

The letter "Å" is actually a later replacement in the Scandinavian languages for "aa." It originated in Sweden in the 16th century before it entered the Norwegian alphabet in 1917 and Danish in 1948. The Icelandic language also uses a form of the letter.

But this isn't a story about absurd grammar, so let's get back to geography!

In the Scandinavian languages, "Å" means "small river" or "stream," so the minuscule place name usually marks a river or a town near a river. Seven villages in Norway are named Å, five villages in Sweden, and one place in Denmark. Perhaps not surprisingly, all of the places named Å tend to be small, just like the name.

It may seem absurd to give a place a one-letter name, but think of how easy it is for the civil servants there to fill out forms? Besides, would you rather tell someone you live in Å or Llanfair-pwllgwyngyllgogerychwyrndrobwllllantysiliogogogoch?

The World's Most Absurdly Scary Bridge

Millions of people around the world suffer from gephyrophobia - the fear of bridges - in varying degrees. It's actually a lot more common than you think, and there's a good chance that plenty of you reading this have experienced it at one point in your life. For most people, gephyrophobia is little more than some sweaty palms or an elevated heartbeat when going over a particularly long, high, and/steep bridge. But for some people, gephyrophobia brings on severe panic attacks.

The anxiety that accompanies driving over a bridge usually begins when the person sees the bridge from a distance and continues on the ascent. Driving up the ascent is usually cited by gephyrophobes as the worst part of the experience, so the higher the gradient, the worst the experience.

A bridge gradient equals a foot in height for every 100 feet in length. The maximum gradient allowed in most places is 12%.

So, let's take a look at what are considered two of the scariest bridges in the world due in large part to their inclines/gradients.

The Rainbow Bridge crosses the Neches River in southeast Texas, connecting that part of Texas to southwestern Louisiana. It is very long and very tall, but what makes it so scary is its approach. The 5% gradient may not sound bad, but it looks terrible from a distance, so much so that people regularly turn around when they see it and decide to drive 45 minutes or more out of their way to get to the other side of the river.

One man was even cited recently for turning around halfway up the ascent, which is one way!

But as scary as the Rainbow Bridge may be, it's got nothing on the Eshima Ohashi Bridge in Japan.

The Eshima Bridge was a major project that began in 1997 and was finally finished in 2004. Once it was done, it connected the people of Matsue with their friends and family in Sakaiminato in southern Japan, but the finished product has left many bridgephobics on either side desperately looking into alternative forms of transportation.

Although images of the bridge circulating on the internet have exaggerated the gradient of the incline, the Matsue side does brag of a fearful 6.1% gradient. In addition to the absurdly steep ascent, the bridge also has a noticeable curve on the Matsue side.

The Eshima Ohashi Bridge may be absurdly scary and a gephyrophobe's worst nightmare, but it serves a purpose and by all accounts is quite stable. So, if you're ever in that part of the world, take a deep breath, relax, and go for a drive over it. What's the worst that can happen?

Alaska and the International Dateline

If you've ever been to Alaska, you know it's a bit of a quirky place. The terrain is rugged, the people are independent, and everything is…big!

Some say that everything in Texas is big, but those who say that have never been to Alaska.

In total area, Alaska is larger than Texas, California, and Montana combined, although it's the least densely populated state and third-least populated state in overall numbers. You can traverse the largely roadless state completely by plane, boat, or snowmobile, and you can theoretically travel for days in Alaska and not see another person. I guess that's part of the charm of Alaska, but it's also one of the reasons for an absurd geographic anomaly.

The Aleutian Islands are that long archipelago that begins on Alaska's southcentral mainland and stretches out for over 1,200 miles into the north Pacific Ocean, covering nearly 7,000 square miles of area. Outside the natives, there aren't many people who live in the Aleutians. The town of Unalaska is the closest thing the islands have to a metropolis, with just over 5,638 (2019) people.

Yes, the Aleutians are a barren, cold place, but they've also been militarily significant in modern times.

The Japanese occupied the westernmost island of Attu during World War II, apparently thinking that it was the gateway to Hollywood or something. The reality is that Attu is closer to Tokyo.

During the Cold War, the Aleutians became an important location for US military bases, as it was located close to Russia where they could spy on the Soviets secretly.

Today, modern technology has made the Cold War techniques of spying with radars and antennas largely obsolete, but the military bases remain in the Aleutians, and the Aleutians are still part of Alaska and the United States.

This brings us to the artificial designation known as the International Date Line and its absurd configuration around the Aleutians.

The International Date Line separates one calendar day from the next *approximately* along the 180° line of longitude. It's approximate as it's subject to change depending upon who controls what, and when.

Here's where things begin to get absurd.

Alaska was originally considered to be west of the Date Line when it was part of the Russian Empire, but when the Russians sold it to the Americans, it was switched to being east of the dateline. So, when Alaska was officially handed over by the Russians to the Americans on October 19, 1867, Alaska technically moved back in time to October 18.

Pretty exciting to get back a lost day, I guess!

Because *all* of Alaska was moved east of the International Date Line, the Aleutians were as well, which today makes for some interesting chronological details, to say the least.

Attu and the western Aleutians are one hour behind the rest of Alaska but a full day behind the Commander Islands, which are closer to 208 miles away. The western Aleutians are also west of other American territories, such as Midway and American Samoa, but an hour ahead in official time.

The good thing about the absurdity of the Aleutians being on the wrong - or the right - side of the International Date Line (I guess that's a matter of perspective), is that the chances of you going there and having to deal with it are quite slim. Attu only has 20 inhabitants (2020), and the entire archipelago has less than 10,000 people.

But if you do go, remember to set your clock *forward*.

You Have to Go through Canada to Get to This Part of Minnesota

Most of the international border between the United States and Canada is set consistently at the 49th parallel. Everything north of that, west of the Great Lakes, is in Canada while everything south is in the US. But obviously, if we're bringing it up in this book, this isn't always the case, so let's take a look at the one absurd exception to this rule...

The Northwest Angle of Minnesota.

The Northwest Angle is the only part of the contiguous western US that is north of the 49th Parallel, but if you ever want to visit the out-of-the-way spot, you'll find it isn't so easy to do. The Angle, as locals call it, is a peninsula surrounded on three sides by the gigantic Lake of the Woods. The only connection it has to the mainland is a road into Manitoba, Canada.

So, if you want to drive to the Angle from Minnesota, you have to take a state highway to the border and then a couple of provincial highways before you get to the Angle and American territory again about one hour later. Once you get to the international border at the Angle, you may be surprised to find that the border patrol station is unstaffed. I guess since only 119 people live in the Angle, there's no urgency from either country to police the border.

There is a booth where, in the most Canadian and northern Minnesotan way, you're politely requested to check-in via videophone.

You can also get there directly from Minnesota if you're a bit more venturesome by air, boat, or on the ice in a snowmobile, car, or truck in the winter.

So how did the geographic absurdity that is the Northwest Angle come to be?

Well, the Treaty of Paris of 1783, which ended the American Revolution, stated that the western boundary between the US and Britain (later Canada) would be from the northwestern shore of the Lake of the Woods, west to the source of the Mississippi River.

The problem is the Mississippi River begins directly south of Lake of the Woods at Lake Itasca and surveyors at the time didn't know how big Lake of the Woods even was. This surveying error was later fixed in 1818 by establishing the international boundary at the 49th Parallel from Lake of the Woods to the Strait of Georgian in British Columbia but trying to keep true to the original intent of the treaty, both sides agreed to keep the Angle in US territory.

Although there have been some who've suggested the Angle should become part of Canada, it seems that the handful of people and plenty of moose who live are there perfectly fine with staying part of the North Star State and the USA.

Islands in Lakes on Islands in Lakes on Islands...

Now I'm going to blow your mind a little bit with a concept that makes you think about things within things, like those Russian nesting dolls where you have one within the other, or how you can take a picture of something within a picture, within a picture...

This same concept of things within other things, getting smaller and smaller, can also be found in geography. It's called recursive islands and lakes. This is pretty weird and a bit absurd when you think about it, but it's also fun.

Let's start with recursive islands. The first level of a recursive island is simply an island in a lake. There are probably millions of these around the world and chances are you know of one.

The next level is an island within an island. Most of these occur on large lakes, with more than 1,000 in Finland alone.

Next are islands in lakes on islands in lakes. There are far fewer of these, obviously, but the largest is Treasure Island (perhaps aptly named) in Canada. So, follow along: Treasure Island is an island on Lake Mindemoya, which is on Manitoulin Island, which is in Lake Huron.

Then there are islands in lakes on islands in lakes on islands, of which there are very few and the smallest islands tend to be extremely small. But if you go to Yathkyed Lake way up near the Arctic Circle in Nunavut, Canada, you'll find the world's only island in a lake on an island in a lake on an island in a lake.

Try saying that more than once fast!

Hopefully, I didn't confuse you too much with the rundown of recursive islands. I confused myself a bit, but now let's take a look at the other side of things - recursive lakes.

The concept with these is essentially the same but instead of starting with an island in a lake, we begin with a lake within an island. As with recursive islands, there are millions of recursive lakes around the world. Pretty much every major island in the world - Ireland, England, New Zealand, and all major islands, for example - have several recursive lakes.

Once we get to the next level of recursive lakes, things there starts to be overlap with recursive islands and things start to get a little confusing. For instance, we go back to Lake Huron to find several lakes on islands in lakes, and Lake Yathkyed has the distinction of having the world's only known lake on an island in a lake on an island in a lake in addition to the world's only island in a lake on an island in a lake on an island in a lake.

I don't know about you, but I'm now totally confused!

The Most **Open** Border in the World

From the United States to Europe, and from Myanmar to Mexico, border security has been a major geopolitical issue in recent years. The debates have surrounded balancing border security and the safety of a nation's citizens with the rights of free travel, trade, and general openness. Border security philosophies tend to change frequently with governments, but there's one place along the US-Canadian border where things haven't changed much in nearly 250 years.

If you ever go to Derby, Vermont or Stanstead, Quebec, be sure to check out Canusa Street to see just how little border security there is.

Canusa Street is not the only street or road in the world that runs along an international border, but it's one of the only ones where the international border is *barely* visible.

It may seem absurd in an era in which drug and human trafficking, terrorism, and mass migration are such big issues, but Canusa Street looks like any other you'd find in America, or Canada, with neatly trimmed lawns, well-kept homes, and two-car driveways - except on this street, one side is in the US while the other is in Canada.

The residents of both sides of Canusa Street - which is obviously named for Canada and USA - take pride in the fact that they are international in their outlook and a symbol of what's possible in the world if we all put our differences aside.

Well, sort of.

Actually, the very practical and pragmatic Quebecers and Vermonters on both sides of Canusa Street don't really look at the big picture much, instead see their neighbors on the other side of the street simply as neighbors. In fact, for much of Canada and the US's history, the border between Derby and Stanstead has been very open, with residents walking back and forth from both sides of the international border, daily, to shop, work, and visit friends and family. There was very little regulation until the September 11 terrorist attacks changed all that.

Now residents are expected to check-in at the border patrol station at the west end of Canusa Street.

But even Canusa Street's border crossing is indicative of the laid-back, easy-going approach to the border by residents of both towns.

The border patrol station on the American side is a small, one-story neo-colonial building that if a border patrol van isn't parked out front can be easily missed among the similar-looking houses and buildings. The Canadian station stands out a bit more, as it is a Tudor-revival structure, but it too blends in well with the Quebec-Vermont landscape.

There have been calls by politicians on both sides of the border to beef up security to limit gun, drug, and people smuggling by closing off streets, but the people of Derby and Stanstead think that'd be absurd!

Strange but True Geography Facts

- Ilha da Queimada Grande, known in English as "Snake Island," is an island about 21 miles off Brazil's coastline that is strictly off-limits to humans. It's home to a large population of golden lancehead pit vipers, so in order to protect the highly venomous snake, as well as humans, the Brazilian government has declared it a no-go zone.

- Taumata¬whakatangihanga¬koauau¬o¬tamatea¬turi¬puka ka¬piki-maunga¬horo¬nuku¬pokai¬whenua¬ki¬tana¬tahu is the longest place name in the world. The 85-letter name is Māori for a hill on New Zealand's North Island. Don't worry, if you're ever there and looking for the place, just ask for it by its better-known abbreviated form, Taumata.

- The Toncontin International Airport in Tegucigalpa, Honduras is another scary airport. The landings are always a real doozy, with pilots being forced to make a sharp turn before landing due to the combination of mountains on one side and the city's skyline all around. Takeoffs are also reportedly white-knuckle-inducing as passengers see the mountains coming at them before gaining altitude. It is only 7,096 feet long (2,163 meters). The airport was built at an elevation of 1,005m (3,294ft).

- Saturn's moon, Titan, is home to reclusive islands, although the liquid is a hydrocarbon.

- The vast majority of the residents of the Norwest Angle are White, but most of the land is owned by the Red Lake Indian Reservation.

- The optical illusion of gravity hills is similar to the Ames room, which is a room that was invented by Adelbert Ames Jr. in 1946. In an Ames room, people seem to grow in size or shrink, as they move around. The effect is the result of a combination of perspective and the irregular shape of the room in a hexahedron.

- Derby Line, Vermont is a village within the town of Derby, Vermont. In Derby Line, you'll find the Haskell Free Library and Opera House, which sits directly on the border, half in the United States, half in Canada.

- Unalaska, Alaska is home to the oldest Russian Orthodox Church in the United States. The Church of the Holy Ascension was first built by the Russians in 1826 and rebuilt by Americans in 1894.

- Angle Inlet is the only town on the Northwest Angle, although it's unincorporated. Lake of the Woods is a popular destination for fishermen from around the world who come to catch walleye, northern pike, muskellunge, and smallmouth bass.

- In addition to having a scary airport, Saba is also home to a potentially active volcano, Mount Scenery. Saba has also been hit by hurricanes in recent years, which present more problems to the island's tourist industry.

CHAPTER 6:

THE ABSURDLY UNEXPLAINED

For the final chapter in our journey through the absurd, we have a sort of hodgepodge of stories that include science, history, geography, true crime, and the supernatural. All of these stories share two important things: they're all pretty weird and they're all unexplained.

Some of these cases are a bit creepy, while others are true mysteries waiting to be solved.

Who knows, maybe you'll be the one to figure it out?

How'd They Make It Back?

Most people love either cats or dogs and there are plenty of people who love both. Cats and dogs seem to bring out the best in people and they're usually there to reciprocate that love and affection.

Well, cats are there to get some food, but that's fine too.

Unfortunately, pet owners will have to face the loss of their beloved pets at some point, sometimes multiple times, and it's never easy. But perhaps worse than a pet dying is one that runs away or gets lost. You never know what happened to Fido or Fluffy and you can only hope that they've found a good home somewhere.

But what about those rare times when they come back?

I know of a guy whose cat got spooked and jumped out of his car about 30 miles from where he lived. He looked and looked but couldn't find his cat so after a few hours he gave up and went home.

Then a few days later, his cat showed up on his doorstep. The cat looked a little beat up from the journey but was in otherwise good health.

This case is by no means unique either.

There's the incredible 1992 case of Sue Anderson and her cat Nova. Sue, her brother, and Sue's four cats packed up a car in Maryland and drove across the country for California. When they were about 200 miles from their destination, Nova went missing. Sue and her brother looked for Nova, but to no avail, so they had to continue to California.

But then a year later Sue was greeted outside her work by a cat that looked surprisingly like Nova. Sue looked the kitty over several times and called its name, coming to the conclusion that it *was* Nova.

Now for all you skeptics out there, I have one more case that proves you can't get between a feline and her home.

In 2013, a cute little tortoiseshell kitty from Florida was on a trip with her family about 200 miles from home when she got spooked and took off (note to cat owners: you probably shouldn't bring your feline friends on long trips!). The family looked for their cat and couldn't find her, so they returned home heartbroken. But two weeks later, they were surprised to get a phone call that their cat had been found in their town by a concerned citizen who brought it to the local vet, who was able to track it back to the family from its chip.

Now that's pretty cool, but it's not just limited to cats.

A collie named Lady was camping with her family, the Riesgrafs, in May 1992 in northern Minnesota when a forest fire caused a quick evacuation of the area. Unfortunately, Lady was left behind and the Riesgraf family thought they had lost her forever.

But two weeks later, they got a call that someone nearby had found her. Lady had traveled more than 150 miles - nearly home!

There are countless other cases where cats and dogs have traveled 100 or more miles across unknown territory to make it home. Scientists are still at a loss to fully explain how it's possible, although, in the case of dogs, it's believed their combination of super smell and the love for their owners drives them home.

For cats, though, I guess you could say it's a bit more cynical.

Cats' super sense is their hearing, so they are possibly helped on their journeys by their ears connecting them to magnetic fields. Overall, cats have a better sense of direction than dogs, but when Fluffy makes it back home after being lost, it's not necessarily because she's drawn to you, but more so her territory.

Some people say it's absurd to think a cat can use its hearing and magnetic fields to function as a sort of living geolocator, and I would agree it certainly *sounds* absurd, but do you have a better explanation?

The World's Most Effective Psychic Detective

When homicide and missing person detectives begin running out of leads on a case, they're often willing to do just about anything. They'll search high and low for new clues and resort to any legal tactic no matter how absurd they may sound.

Absurd-sounding tactics...like using psychics.

Police departments generally prefer to solve cases with tried-and-true investigation methods, but sometimes they'll take whatever help they can get, including psychics. But as absurd as psychics helping the cops may sound, it's been done for decades around the world.

And none have been more successful than American Nancy Myer.

Nothing about Nancy Myer's background screams "psychic." She was born in New York state, traveled the world with her father who was in the foreign service and earned a BA in Spanish from the University of Delaware. Although Nancy mastered Spanish and taught it at the college level, it was her other "gift" that made her famous.

Nancy realized or claims that she was given, the gift of clairvoyance and the ability to see events that had already taken place or were taking place at the time but in another location. She eventually brought her gift to various police departments on the East Coast in the 1990s but was met with varying degrees of skepticism.

Myer claims she's consulted police departments on more than 300 cases, giving useful clues in 80% of those. She's also claimed to have consulted with hundreds of private individuals and families, helping them find lost items and loved ones. Although it's difficult to confirm these numbers, there are a few notable cases where police and private individuals have claimed that indeed Nancy Myer did help crack a case.

Nancy's most high-profile case came when a serial rapist was stalking the streets of Wilmington, Delaware. Unable to make any headway with the case, Wilmington detective Leroy Landon gave Nancy a call to see if she could "see" anything.

Nancy met with the rape victims and afterwards started having visions of a particular Wilmington neighborhood. After doing some good old-fashioned police work, Landon was able to narrow things down to a halfway house, and after interviewing the residents, they eventually caught the rapist.

Myer has also located missing people, alive and dead, who disappeared under various circumstances.

For example, in 1988, 76-year-old Sylvester Tonet wandered off from his rural Monroeville, Pennsylvania home. Sylvester's family looked for him but soon called the local police, who also failed to locate the senior citizen.

Finally, the local police contacted Nancy Myer for help.

Nancy went into a "trance" and retold in detail how Sylvester became disorientated and died of exposure. She then accurately described where his body was within 150 yards.

Skeptics say that Nancy Myer has gotten "lucky" on her many successful cases, but I think that's absurd. There's obviously something more going on with her and other, similar psychic detectives, although what *it* exactly is will probably forever remain a mystery of the universe.

Nazi UFOs or St. Elmo's Fire?

Toward the end of World War II, Allied pilots flying over Europe and the Pacific were sometimes greeted with a strange phenomenon that remains unexplained, with many of the explanations offered being considered quite absurd. Pilots reported seeing balls of light they described as "Christmas tree lights" and "fireballs" that seemed to have a life of their own, descending and ascending and occasionally *following* the pilots through the skies.

These strange lights became known as foo fighters (yes, that overrated '90s band took their name from this phenomenon) and have since become the subject of continual debate.

So, what did the pilots see and what are some of the possible explanations for this phenomenon?

Pilots in the US Army's 415th Night Fighter Squadron were among the first to report seeing these strange, bright lights over Europe. The origin of the term "foo fighters", though, is almost as much of a mystery as the phenomenon itself. Some believe the term came from a slang term used in a newspaper comic from the 1930s, while others think it was an abbreviation of the popular acronym used at the time: FUBAR, which means, "f*cked up beyond all recognition."

The bright, seemingly sentient lights ended as soon as the war did, leading many to believe that the explanation had to do with the war. It was also curious that most of the sightings began toward the end of the war, leading to what many believe is the most plausible explanation.

Both the Germans and Japanese were experimenting with some pretty interesting aerial weapons at that stage. The Germans put the first fighter jets in the sky and sent the first rockets - the V1 and the V2 - roaring over Europe.

Although the Japanese didn't develop jets or rockets, they did create "bomb balloons", which were giant helium balloons capable of traveling thousands of miles before crashing and exploding.

It's likely that at least on a few occasions Allied pilots saw rockets, jets, and bomb balloons traveling through the night skies.

But that doesn't explain all or probably even most foo fighter sightings.

In 1952, the US government created the Robertson Panel to investigate the sightings. You probably already know the conclusion the Panel came to, but I'll tell you anyway.

The Robertson Panel "concluded" that the lights weren't a threat, and they weren't sentient. The Panel stated that all sightings could be written off as natural phenomena including reflections from objects or St. Elmo's fire.

Of course, not all witnesses of foo fighters agreed with these explanations, but what can you do when it's a government panel? Case closed, right?

Well, things then got handed off to the conspiracy theorists to come up with the real fun and often most absurd explanations.

The most obvious explanation to the conspiracy buffs is that the foo fighters were really extra-terrestrials, possibly warning humans about the dire consequences of a world war. This may work for some, but for many others, the Nazi-UFO theory is the best.

According to the Nazi-UFO theory, the foo fighters were actually Nazi secret weapons, possibly extra-terrestrial (I guess that means some aliens liked the Nazis), although not necessarily.

There are several problems with this last theory, though. Why would the Nazis wait so long to unleash such badass technology? Also, if the technology was so badass, why didn't it take down a single Allied plane?

I guess that puts us right back to where we started and the likelihood that the truth behind the foo fighters will never be known.

The Lost Dutchman's Mine

It's absurd to think we'll ever just randomly stumble across a fortune, right? I mean, that's something we may dream about, and something you see in movies, but not something that happens in real life.

How many people do you know who've found a fortune in the walls of their home?

Do you know anyone who's found a lost treasure?

I don't either, but the reality is that if you somehow did beat the absurd odds by finding a fortune, would you tell anyone about it?

That's the background of our next unexplained absurd case. For this one, we travel to the picturesque Superstition Mountains in Arizona, where the mystery of a supposedly hidden treasure has been ongoing for more than 100 years.

The story begins in the late 1800s when a German immigrant named Jakob Waltz supposedly discovered the stash but kept his mouth shut about its location, apparently taking the secret with him to the grave in 1891. Due to Waltz's German background (the German word for German is "Deutsch," so Germans were often incorrectly called "Dutch" in the US at that time), the legendary stash became known as the Dutchman's Mine. The story of the origins of the loot, how it got there, and even the existence of Waltz himself has had numerous variations over the years.

Some say the treasure was originally Spanish gold that was taken by Apache Indians, while others say the gold originally belonged to the Apache. Some versions say that American soldiers stashed the gold, and others say that Waltz had a partner who he may or may not have killed!

No one knows the truth for sure, but what we do know is that several people have died trying to find the Dutchman's Mine.

The first notable death associated with the mine, and the one that started the legend and talk of a curse, was that of Adolph Ruth. Ruth left his home in 1931 in search of the mine and was never heard from again. Not alive, anyway.

A skull and human remains were later discovered with some of Ruth's personal belongings. A forensic examination of the skull revealed that Ruth had been shot in the head, but the local authorities ruled that it was probably self-inflicted. Skeptics point out that the pistol discovered near Ruth's remains was fully loaded.

There was also an ominous note found near Ruth's remains that claimed he'd found the lost treasure.

Was Adolph Ruth murdered for the treasure of the Lost Dutchman's Mine?

This is one of those enigmas enclosed in a mystery accompanied by a paradox (the unfired suicide weapon), but it was only the beginning of the legend of the Lost Dutchman's Mine. Ruth's death/murder only helped the legend grow and brought more and more people to the Superstition Mountains to find the mine.

And several others would meet the same fate as Ruth.

A man named James Cravey set out to find the Dutchman's Mine in the 1940s and was never heard from again. His severed head was later discovered, but it was never determined how he lost it!

More recently, in 2011, the remains of three men who set out to find the Dutchman's Mine in 2010 were discovered. The local authorities stated they probably died of heat exhaustion, but many people believe they were the victims of a curse.

In the end, it all comes down to perspective when you talk about the Lost Dutchman's Mine. You can choose to believe any of the numerous origin stories, or if the treasure is cursed or not. You can also choose to believe that the entire story is absurd.

Overdose or Organized Crime Hit?

It's really absurd how far a celebrity or wealthy person can fall after being at the top of their game. Every now and then, we read about a celebrity or famous person who had it all and then blew it all, often thanks to drugs, alcohol, or bad business deals.

The demise of these people can usually be seen a mile away, but sometimes the final details remain forever an absurd mystery.

In 1962, Sonny Liston was at the top of the world. As the world heavyweight boxing champ, he had fame, money, and a career that appeared to be on a steady upward trajectory. But on December 30, 1970, it all ended at his home in Las Vegas, Nevada.

The local police said Liston died of a heroin overdose, but his wife, many of his friends, and those he worked with, in the boxing world, said that was impossible. Liston didn't do heroin and he was extremely afraid of needles.

So, what or who killed Sonny Liston?

The potential answer to that question can only be found in Liston's tough life and sometimes shady background.

A lot of mystery surrounds Sonny Liston's life. The exact year he was born is even disputed. Liston claimed he was born in 1932 in the tiny town of Sand Slough, Arkansas, but some historians believe it may have been 1930. Whatever the year, Liston started life during the Great Depression in the era of racial segregation in the Deep South to an abusive father.

After Liston's mother took part of the family to St. Louis, Missouri, Sonny stayed in Arkansas until he was around 12 before joining his mother.

But young Sonny learned that although he didn't face the same level of poverty and discrimination in St. Louis as he did in Arkansas, things were tougher in a different sort of way. Liston began running with a street gang and before too long, he racked up a series of violent crime convictions and was sentenced to time in the state prison.

It was while he was in prison that Liston learned how to box. After Liston got out, he boxed in amateur leagues for a bit before quickly moving up into the pros.

But the life of the streets was never far from Liston.

Liston regularly rubbed shoulders with organized crime figures in St. Louis, Philadelphia, and Las Vegas, as it was mobsters who financed his early career. In the early days, Liston also moonlighted as a mob enforcer and "collections specialist."

And as Liston moved up the ranks to get his title shot against Floyd Patterson on September 25, 1962, controversy about his criminal record and organized crime ties followed him.

Liston remained the champ until he was defeated by a young up-and-comer named Cassius Clay (better known later as Muhammad Ali). After a tough six rounds, Liston failed to emerge from his corner for the seventh round and Clay was declared the winner by technical knockout.

There was talk that Liston threw the fight, but that was just murmurs, the most part. Anyone who saw the fight knew it was tough and could've gone either way. It was the rematch that really made people wonder just how deep Liston was involved with organized crime.

Liston-Clay II took place on May 25, 1965, in Lewiston, Maine. The site was moved from the original location of Boston due to concerns of ties to organized crime in that city, but the change of venue didn't seem to matter. Liston was knocked out in the first round in what many today say was one of the most obvious flops in sports history.

Liston attempted a comeback after Ali's title was vacated for him refusing to enter the military draft, but the former champ never got another chance.

Liston's wife found his body in their bedroom. The police found three small bags of heroin in the kitchen and about an ounce of marijuana.

But here's where things get absurd.

The coroner only found trace amounts of codeine and morphine in Liston's system, not nearly enough for an overdose. And although a needle mark was found on his arm, those close to him believe it was from a hospital visit he had a month earlier.

And Liston's wife and friends all pointed out that he hated needles to the point of canceling a trip to Africa that would've required vaccinations.

Because of all this, many people have theorized that Sonny's ties to organized crime finally caught up with him. Some think he was killed for not throwing Liston-Clay II in a convincing enough manner, or that when he wasn't paid for throwing the fight, he threatened to go public with details about the dive.

Another theory is that Liston was supposed to take a dive in his last career fight against Chuck Wepner in June 1970. After beating the tar out of Wepner for more than nine rounds, Liston was dead just a few months later.

Other theories have Liston working for local Las Vegas mobsters as a bag man and running afoul of them when he tried to go independent or being labeled a snitch by Las Vegas drug dealers.

With all of these theories, the story goes that the killers got Liston drunk - Sonny Liston wasn't a known drug user, but he was known to be a heavy drinker - and then shot a lethal amount of heroin into his arm. The killers then took the needle, spoon, and tourniquet (none of which were found at the Liston home) before leaving.

But the problem with this theory - and even an accidental overdose theory, for that matter - is the trace amounts of opioids found in Liston's system weren't enough to kill him. Unfortunately, it seems that the case of Sonny Liston's death is so absurdly strange that it will never be truly solved.

The Disappearance and Reappearance of Steven Kubacki

Every year about 600,000 people go missing in the United States. The vast majority of those people return home, or turn up somewhere, with most of them being juveniles and young adults who ran away from home for a variety of reasons.

And then there are the people who are sick of their middle-class lives and want to experience something different. They too usually return home after a few days or weeks once they've seen that the grass isn't necessarily always greener on the other side.

But then there are the less than 100,000 active missing persons cases. Many of them will also return to their homes, but their cases are usually a little more complicated. Heavy drug use, human trafficking, or mental illness are often the reasons behind these long-term missing persons cases. Many are tragic, some are strange, but none are as absurd as our next case.

In late February 1978, a 23-year-old Hope College senior named Steven Kubacki disappeared near the eastern shore of Lake Michigan. He had left for a short cross-country skiing outing as he often did in the winter, but when he didn't return, his family and friends called the police. A search revealed his skis, backpack, and a 200-yard path of footprints in the snow that led to a frozen lake.

110

The local authorities concluded that Kubacki probably fell through the ice and had drowned.

Kubacki's family, friends, and fellow students at the small Christian college were devastated but refused to believe he was dead. He was an avid outdoorsman who had a lot to live for, including a potential job at a local newspaper, and his family's home was about to be signed over to him.

The Kubacki family hired private detectives who sent Steven's dental records to Illinois to have them checked against those of serial killer John Wayne Gacy's unidentified victims. Steven was luckily not one of Gacy's victims, but what happened next is almost as creepy.

Kubacki reportedly "woke up" on May 5, 1979, in a field near Pittsfield, Massachusetts, about 700 miles from his Michigan home. He walked to a family member's home nearby and was shortly thereafter reunited with the rest of his family and greeted by the press.

But Kubacki had little to say about his missing 14 months.

He had a backpack with items from around the country, which included a t-shirt from a marathon in Wisconsin.

What happened to Steven Kubacki remains a mystery. He had no problems moving on with his life, though, becoming a psychologist and writing a book titled *Meta-Mathematical Foundations of Existence: Gödel, Quantum, God & Beyond*. Since his initial interviews with the press, Kubacki has refused to comment on his odyssey.

Cynics say Kubacki made the whole thing up, while others think it was some sort of stress-induced psychosis. Perhaps the most absurd explanation is that he was the victim of the "Great Lakes/Lake Michigan Triangle", which is thought to be a supernatural vortex that sucks people, planes, and ships into it just like the Bermuda Triangle.

Whatever the explanation, Steven Kubacki's is one of the strangest disappearance cases in history.

The Mystery of the Missing Feet, or is it Missing Bodies?

On August 20, 2007, an American girl visiting Jedediah Island in British Columbia, Canada saw something on the beach that caught her eye. If you've ever spent time on a beach, you know that a lot of strange items wash up and it can be quite fun, especially for kids, finding these things.

Maybe you'll find an old beer bottle from 20 years ago.

You could find some rare coins.

Or…how about a human foot?

Well, I think it's safe to say that most of us wouldn't think finding a human foot on the beach as a "score," but when that girl found a foot, it opened the case on a macabre and absurd mystery that's lasted for several years.

The foot, which was a size 12, was still in a sneaker. Its accompanying foot was nowhere to be found, nor was the body that originally came with it. The authorities were at a loss, but just six days later, another foot washed up on another British Columbian island.

Then more feet started washing up on various islands in British Columbia and Washington state's Puget Sound. Eventually, more than 21 cases of disarticulated feet were recorded, which frightened the public and gave the conspiracy theorists plenty of grist.

Was it someone who took a foot fetish too far, like an evil podiatrist?

Maybe it was some type of Satanic cult that was taking body parts and for whatever leaving the feet.

By 2017, the authorities reported they had most of the cases solved. The bodies of nearly every foot had been accounted for in suicides and accidents near the water. Experts said that once the bodies were in the water, natural decomposition took over and the feet became disarticulated from the rest of the body.

Experts also stated that it's unheard of for so many feet of drowning and/or suicide victims to turn up on shore. The feet usually sink to the bottom and never come up or they are eaten by fish or other scavengers.

If that's the case, how why were so many feet found on the islands of British Columbia and Washington from 2007 to 2019? Experts believe the answer to that is that nearly all of the feet were wearing sneakers, which gave the feet buoyancy.

Still, the experts also say that finding two feet washed up on shore, never mind nearly two dozen, is a one in a million chance. It really makes you wonder if something more is going on up there.

Cryptic Message or Elaborate Hoax?

Since the first words were written on papyrus, and clay tablets, more than 5,000 years ago, writing has been a combination of art and science. People developed writing systems to accommodate their specific languages, and over time, those systems were adopted by other people. And as the world got smaller thanks to inventions and technologies that allow people from around the world to communicate almost instantly, the many different forms of writing, and languages, became less mysterious.

All of the modern languages and their accompanying written scripts were known by the late 1800s and early 1900s, so scholars began decoding the languages of the past, such as ancient Egyptian hieroglyphs, the different forms of cuneiform, and even the Mayan language to just name three.

But in 1912, a Polish scholar named Wilfrid Voynich threw a monkey wrench in academia when he produced an approximately 240-page manuscript that was written in an unknown script.

Scholars attempted to translate what became known as the Voynich manuscript but to no avail. Only a few pages could be identified as using the Latin script, although most are written in an unknown alphabet that uses no punctuation.

As news of the Voynich manuscript made the rounds and academics examined it, some declared it an absurd forgery.

But a forgery of what?

The artistic style of the accompanying pictures looked to be late medieval European, and the arrangement of the book seemed to be that of a pharmacological text, so it would seem to be a lot of work for a simple forgery. Plus, there's been no known book found on which it could have been based.

So, the Voynich manuscript lingered for decades in obscurity, moving from private hands until it was donated to Yale University in 1969. Not long after, there was a renewed interest in the bizarre manuscript thanks in part to historical research and new technology. Historians discovered that the earliest known owner of the manuscript was a 17th-century Czech alchemist and antiquities dealer named Georg Baresch.

It is believed that the next owner was 17th-century philologist Jesuit Athanasius Kircher. Apparently, the Jesuits later sold the book, along with many others, to private sellers, which is how Voynich got a hold of it.

Even with all that detailed genealogy, some still thought the most obvious explanation was the answer - that Voynich wrote the book himself.

Although Voynich was a smart guy with a background in pharmacology and languages, a major twist came in 2009 when a team from the University of Arizona carbon-tested part of the manuscript. The test revealed that at least the vellum (the material of the pages) was from the early 1400s. Further tests revealed that the ink was consistent with that period as well.

So, this brings everything back to the beginning.

Expert code breakers have attempted to crack the code of the manuscript but to no avail, and philologists have offered a range of theories, from it being a known Asian language written in a contrived script to a Germanic language also in a contrived script. Others believe it was a shorthand of Latin or Greek.

Others believe it is written in a constructed language like Esperanto, discussed previously in this book.

And the hoax/forgery idea keeps resurfacing. In 1978, an American professor named Robert Brumbaugh even made the claim that the manuscript was faked and intended to be sold to Rudolf II, the Holy Roman Emperor (ruled 1576-1612 CE).

Since the 1920s, people have claimed to have translated at least part of the book, but none of their claims has been accepted by academia. Some of the claims have been more absurd than others and as time goes on and the Voynich manuscript remains undeciphered, I'm sure the absurd claims will continue.

Strange but True Unexplained Facts

- St. Elmo's fire is created when a corona discharge from an object creates a luminous discharge that is usually blue or purple. The effect is named for St. Erasmus of Formia who noted that the effect could indicate an impending lightning strike. As cool as St. Elmo's fire looks, though, I'm not sure how it could be confused with a UFO.

- Nancy Weber is another notable psychic who worked with police departments in New Jersey to solve a number of cases, such as the murder of Elizabeth Cornish. The police initially focused on Cornish's boyfriend until Weber told them she had a vision of a very specific man who lived next door to the victim. After investigating the psychic lead, the police discovered that Weber was right!

- Former Alaska US Senator Ted Stevens reported seeing a foo fighter, or something, when he was flying a mission for the US Army Air Force over Europe in World War II.

- Although Sonny Liston was left-handed, he fought in the "orthodox" style (left foot forward), which is much more common among right-handed boxers.

- An episode of the police procedural drama *Bones* "tackled" the topic of the disarticulated feet washing ashore in British Columbia and Washington.

- The Great Lakes have long been the subject of mysteries going back to the Indigenous tribes that lived on their shores before the Europeans. The mysterious sinking of the *Edmund Fitzgerald* on November 10, 1975, on Lake Superior is notable, but other planes, smaller boats, and people have mysteriously disappeared on the Great Lakes, especially the western lakes. Steven Kubacki, though, is the only known case to have "come back" from wherever it was he went.

- Although this is not official, a cat named Sugar is said to have traveled over 1,500 miles from Anderson, California to Gage, Oklahoma to unite with its owners. It took Sugar 14 months to complete her journey.

- Yale University is also home to the *Vinland Map*, which was once believed to be a 15th-century version of an earlier Viking map that showed the "New World." In 2018, based on the detection of modern ink, the map was determined to be a hoax.

- Although many treasure hunters have died trying to find the Lost Dutchman's Mine, hundreds or more have unsuccessfully attempted to find the treasure but lived. Among those who struck out on the gold but lived to tell the tale, was Robert Corbin, a former Attorney General for the state of Arizona.

- Perhaps the most absurd explanation for the foo fighters' phenomenon is that the UFOs were secret Nazi technology (in some versions extraterrestrial in origin) that was stored under Antarctica. In case you're wondering why Antarctica (as am I), it's because there is an opening there to "hollow Earth." You can't make this stuff up!

CONCLUSION

I hope you enjoyed our journey through some of the most absurd events, people, places, and things in the world. We've looked at historical and scientific absurdities, ventured into the always absurd world of pop culture, examined the strangest things in literature and art, visited some of the wackiest places on Earth, and finished it off some of the most absurd and unexplained cases of strangeness known to humanity.

In addition to having fun and getting a kick out of this book, I bet you learned a thing or two, not just about these specific cases but about the world in general.

I like to think that all of these stories demonstrate just how absurd life can be and that sometimes when everything around us seems so serious, it helps to take a break and just have a laugh about things. Sometimes even at others' expense!

The idea of chastity belts, the background of the hyena, and the idea that Paul McCartney was replaced with a double are all silly things that are fun to talk about and have a good laugh. Thinking about them can help us make it through the day or even serve as an ice breaker at your next tense business meeting or family get-together.

Another thing I hope you learned is that one person's absurdity may be another person's revelation, treasure, or cure. Eating cockroaches may seem like an absurd cure for ailments to you, but to others, they seemingly work wonders.

So, the next time you see or hear about something that seems so absurd you wonder how it's even possible, or how someone could even come up with the idea, know that it may make the next volume of this book!